Risking Intensity

Risking Intensity

Reading and
Writing Poetry
with High School Students

Judith Rowe Michaels

Princeton Day School

National Council of Teachers of English
1111 W. Kenyon Road, Urbana, Illinois 61801-1096

Staff Editor: Zarina M. Hock
Interior Design: Barbara Yale-Read
Cover Design: Barbara Yale-Read

NCTE Stock Number: 41714-3050

Library of Congress Cataloging-in-Publication Data
Michaels, Judith Rowe, 1944–
    Risking intensity: reading and writing poetry with high school students/Judith Rowe Michaels.
       p.   cm.
    Includes bibliographical references (p.).
    ISBN 0-8141-4171-4 (pbk.)
    1. Poetry—Study and teaching (Secondary) 2. Poetry—Authorship. 3. School verse, American. I. Title.
PN1101.M48 1999
808.1—dc21   98-47499
                                                   CIP

To my husband, Bill Michaels

Contents

Foreword

The narrative voice in this lovely book is that of a poet who happens to be a teacher. She is a skilled poet, a committed poet, still in search of herself; and she communicates to young people as well as to her readers what it signifies to be in process, to be in quest. At once, she is the kind of teacher who understands how to release her students' varied voices, how to break through the blocks and silences. In the pages to follow, readers are enabled to witness Judith Michaels's efforts to move varied young people to write poetry in an ongoing interchange with a teacher who is reading and writing along with them.

The voices sound and resound in an open-ended conversation, not only between teacher and learners, but within a wondrous gathering of poets ranging from William Blake to Adrienne Rich to Quincy Troupe. The poets are chosen if their themes and concerns mesh, at a certain moment, with those that have caught the attention of the young people and their teacher: memory, it may be; the shapes of childhood; the physicality of the self; relationships; fear and anger; politics, justice, rejection, community. Nothing is explicitly demanded: there are models, instances of what might be. Nothing is imposed on those who resist or avert their eyes: there is always an alternative possibility so long as a writer will risk what Judith Michaels calls "intensity."

Reading, savoring young people's poems, their teachers' poems, great poets' poems, this reader recalls the closing pages of Toni Morrison's *Beloved.* Paul D is recalling an old friend's effort to describe a woman he loved: "She is a friend of my mind. She gather me, man. The pieces I am, she gather them and give them back to me in all the right order. It's good, you know, when you got a woman who is a friend of your mind." Judith Michaels, always becoming, chooses herself as a friend of her students' minds. It needs to be said that she is insistent on young persons developing a reflective and critical approach to their own work, to their own listening and paying heed. If teaching of the sort explored in this book is indeed a mode of friendship, the acts of teaching do not allow the young to stay comfortably where they are. Like John Dewey, this teacher reaches out to empower youngsters to become different—to see further, to imagine with more ardor, to confront contradiction, to make increasing sense of the world around.

Poetry is the mode of their becoming; and the teacher extends their reach and her own as they venture into different communities beyond Princeton Day School, where Judith Michaels teaches, to come in touch with different young people, different realities. Poetry, too, becomes a mode of engaging with different modes of literature, indeed with the range of art forms the young are helped to bring to life. When the time comes (and only then) there are the critical and the analytic texts, but only when the young people can be helped by them in their search for what might be called a poetic literacy.

Having worked for years in teacher education, struggled to find texts that capture the music (yes, and the dissonances) of live classrooms, I find this book by an authentic literary artist to be as generative of good ideas for teaching as some of the best studies of classroom *praxis:* Donald Schon's, for instance, Eleanor Duckworth's, Vivian Paley's, Courtney Cazden's. There are few practitioners who can, so graciously and passionately, open a world to young people and, at once, pursue the daily life of teaching high school. There is even talk of portfolios in this book, portfolios introduced as a step on the way of learning the craft of poetry. Judith Michaels's ongoing journey takes her beyond; it takes her, hand in hand with her student friends, into the inexhaustible regions of art. Nothing in this book can be subsumed under words like "rubric" or even "domain"; we enter the realm of the possible, not the predictable. We may well find ourselves walking often with this book in hand. We cannot but feel (we who are teachers) that, having sensed a new beginning, we have found a remarkable friend.

Maxine Greene

Professor Emerita of Philosophy and Education,
Teachers College, Columbia University
Philosopher-in-Residence, Lincoln Center
Institute for the Arts in Education

Acknowledgments

My thanks to Princeton Day School for helping me create the position of artist-in-residence, which allowed me some time for working on this book, and for their summer grants that enabled me to accept writing residencies at Cottages at Hedgebrook and the Banff Centre for the Arts. Thanks in particular to the Banff Centre, where for three summers this book took shape.

I also owe a great deal to the Geraldine R. Dodge Foundation, whose poetry program for high school students in New Jersey made available to me the work as well as live readings of poets I might otherwise never have known and gave me colleagues among poets and poetry teachers from whom I have learned a great deal.

Thanks also to Molly Peacock, in whose poetry workshop I first discovered how to give and receive constructive criticism and what contemporary poets were doing with formal verse.

I thank Dr. Maxine Greene for the wisdom and passion of her summer lectures on aesthetic education at the Lincoln Center Institute, in all of which she quoted poetry, and also for the informal discussions she offered at her home.

Like most teachers, I owe a lot to my students, not only those of high school age, some of whose writing I have quoted in this book, but also the younger ones with whom I recently began to work as artist-in-residence at my kindergarten through twelfth-grade school.

And I must thank the faithful poet correspondent whose suggestions through the mail have strengthened my poems as well as my teaching—my Detroit connection, Terry Blackhawk.

I owe much to my parents for their knowledge of music and their love of poetry; and above all I am grateful to my husband for the wide range of his reading in contemporary poetry and his willingness to read and offer suggestions about my own writing.

Permissions

Chapter 1

Risking Intensity

*IF THERE WERE NO POETRY ON ANY DAY IN THE WORLD, POETRY WOULD BE
INVENTED THAT DAY. FOR THERE WOULD BE AN INTOLERABLE HUNGER.
AND FROM THAT NEED, FROM THE RELATIONSHIPS WITHIN OURSELVES AND
AMONG OURSELVES AS WE WENT ON LIVING, AND FROM EVERY OTHER
EXPRESSION OF MAN'S NATURE, POETRY WOULD BE—I CANNOT HERE SAY
INVENTED OR DISCOVERED—POETRY WOULD BE DERIVED. AS RESEARCH
SCIENCE WOULD BE DERIVED, IF THE ENERGIES WE NOW BEGIN TO KNOW
REDUCED US TO A FEW PEOPLE, RUBBING INTO LIFE A LITTLE FIRE.*

MURIEL RUKEYSER, *THE LIFE OF POETRY*

In general, teachers are not expected to lay bare their hearts in the
classroom. Most students—and I was one of these—have little access to their
teachers' emotions. They don't picture us in mourning, in love, in doubt,
fighting with our parents and children, excited about vacations. They're
even amazed when they catch us buying groceries or going to the movies. If

we stop to brush away tears while reading aloud Virginia Woolf's suicide
note, their initial reaction is acute embarrassment. So is ours—and perhaps
we resolve never to run such a risk again.

Poets, on the other hand, are expected to give voice to what they feel.
Galway Kinnell, whose poems reflect a struggle to be honest about the
heart's affections, offers the age-old justification for doing this: "The more
deeply, truly personal your poem, the more likely it will be universal,
touching a level in the psyche where we're all the same."[1]

But what if both teacher and student are afraid to be touched? Then we
are also likely to be afraid of poetry.

Add to this fear the fact that poetry was initially presented to many of
us as something to "tear apart" in order to find the single correct "hidden
meaning" possessed by the teacher, and it's hardly surprising if we distrust
it. Even though we now know the answers to "Ode on a Grecian Urn." Or
perhaps we feel as we often do about being parents: "I'm not going to make
the same mistakes. . . ." A tall order! No wonder we steer clear of poetry.

I'm a teacher; we're supposed to have answers. To what a poem means;
to whether it's great or merely good; to why we should read poetry at all; to
what's on the next test, where we are going, and where we have been. But
I'm also a poet; and poetry, as Lucille Clifton has said, is all about questions.
These past ten years of writing poems have often forced me to question
what I used to believe were perfectly good answers.

Which seems to me like a fine reason to write poetry. And it certainly
makes teaching poems easier—not feeling that you have to have all the
answers. I'm repeatedly struck by what wonderfully *unanswerable* questions a good poem asks our minds to entertain.

The mind, though we tend to forget this, is also the nervous system. So
poetry speaks to the body. And this is probably another source of our dis-
comfort with it. The body is no more acceptable in our classrooms than the
emotions or the unanswerable question. The body was made to sit quietly at
a desk and take notes. But once you begin writing poems and rediscover
your five senses, your nerves, the way your pulse races and your hands get
cold with excitement when images start to emerge on the page and a
blurred memory comes suddenly into focus, you may find yourself struggling with a whole new vision of what you want the classroom to be.

My vision expanded further when I began giving workshops in elementary schools. It was only when my senior poetry class insisted, after visiting

our first graders, "We gotta have a rabbit!" that I knew a moment's hesitation.

So here we are in class with no feelings, no body, no unanswerable questions, no rabbit—and no time. How, in our daily rush to cover the texts, to prepare for tests, to prepare for college, can we possibly make a quiet space inside our students and ourselves where we can be touched, where we can receive or create a poem on breath, pulse, and nerves? Where we can entertain unanswerable questions.

Reading and writing poems can help us discover profound truths we didn't realize we knew. It can waken our senses and empathy, so we really begin to see a new world. It can help us to know ourselves better. And offer solace for the pain of that self-knowledge. But no quick worksheet or training in writing analytical essays can make this happen; nor can the fear of a test or the desire for college acceptance or a better job motivate our students to open themselves to the muse.

I think we all suspect, in our heart of hearts, that the enjoyment of poetry has something to do with our capacities for dreaming, remembering, and play. But how to create an inclination to encounter the self in these ways within the confines of the traditional school day and curriculum? And how to assess these encounters? Can one grade a dream? A game? A memory?

A sixteen-year-old girl told me recently, "When people write poems they are putting themselves on the line—to be criticized or praised. It is really risky. For me to write a decent poem, I must release all inhibitions, and then go with it." Adrienne Rich, activist and poet, recognizes the risk, but insists:

> *You must write, and read, as if your life depended on it.* That is not
> generally taught in school. At most, *as if your livelihood depended on
> it:* the next step, the next job . . . no questions asked as to further
> meanings. And, let's face it, the lesson of the schools for a vast
> number of children—hence, of readers—is *This is not for you.*
>   To read as if your life depended on it would mean to let into your
> reading your beliefs, the swirl of your dreamlife, the physical
> sensations of your ordinary carnal life; and, simultaneously, to
> allow what you're reading to pierce the routines, safe and imperme-
> able, in which ordinary carnal life is tracked, charted, channeled.
> . . . Or, you can say: 'I don't understand poetry.'[2]

Risking Intensity invites you to try discovering and writing poems along with your students and, in the process, to find out together what "safe and impermeable routines" need to be pierced in order to write and read as if your life depended on it.

At my writing table, in my classroom, and in other teachers' classes where I've worked as visiting poet, there is one thing I've invariably found to be true: Because good poems speak to the heart, they create a sense of community. It doesn't matter whether they're classic or contemporary, written by teacher or student. And for the same reason, sharing poems can *widen* this community—can help us find commonality with people outside our own circle.

Discovering commonality—among different ages, cultures, and races seems to me one of the most important tasks for student and teacher. As I write this, I glance out of my studio window at the field and trees of a breathtakingly beautiful park in the Canadian Rockies and remember Bertolt Brecht's uncomfortable question:

> *What kind of times are they, when*
> *A talk about trees is almost a crime*
> *Because it implies silence about so many horrors?*[3]

And, fresh from reading Jonathan Kozol's *Savage Inequalities*,[4] I think about the teacher in East St. Louis, faced with two hundred twelfth-graders who are expected—in theory—to compete for college places or jobs with privileged private school students yet have too few textbooks, no computers, and one-fifth of a guidance counselor. I think about the teacher whose thirty first-graders share a decaying gym with three other classes—all children whose poverty and races have doomed them to live in a dangerously polluted part of the city, too close to a flooding river—children who can't concentrate because of malnutrition. Is poetry, whether written in forests or on subways, powerful enough to penetrate these horrors? To bridge such chasms? I don't know. I can only put my trust in Galway Kinnell's words and hope that my experiences and those of my students go deep enough to reach that "level in the psyche where we're all the same."

Notes

1. Galway Kinnell in "The Simple Acts of Life," writ. James Haba and Ann Price, *The Power of the Word with Bill Moyers: A Six-Part Series of Contemporary Poetry* (New York: PBS VIDEO, David Grubin Productions, 1989). This is a wonderful series of conversations and poetry readings, on four videotapes that include footage from one of the Geraldine R. Dodge Poetry Festivals at Waterloo, New Jersey. It brings "live" to the classroom some highly accessible contemporary poets, such as Sharon Olds, Lucille Clifton, Quincy Troupe, Joy Harjo, Gerald Stern, Garrett Hongo, Li-Young Lee, Stanley Kunitz, Robert Bly, and the late Mary TallMountain.

2. Adrienne Rich, *What Is Found There: Notebooks on Poetry and Politics* (New York: W. W. Norton, 1993) 32–33. A book that should live by your bed, except that it will keep you awake with its passionate commitment to change the world through writing and reading poetry. The title comes from a passage in William Carlos Williams's "Asphodel, That Greeny Flower": "It is difficult / to get the news from poems / yet men die miserably every day / for lack / of what is found there."

3. Bertolt Brecht, "Bad Time for Poetry," trans. John Willet and Ralph Manheim, cited by David Mura, "On Poetry and Politics: Brecht, Rich, and C. K. Williams," *AWP Chronicle*, 23.3 (Norfolk, VA: Associated Writing Programs, 1990) 2. AWP is an organization of college creative writing programs, but anyone can subscribe to their publication and the articles are sometimes relevant to high school poetry teachers.

4. Jonathan Kozol, *Savage Inequalities* (New York: HarperCollins, 1991).

Chapter 2

The Start: Writing Your Own Poem

PRACTICE OF AN ART IS MORE SALUTARY THAN TALK ABOUT IT.
THERE IS NOTHING MORE COMPOSING THAN COMPOSITION.

ROBERT FROST, FROM HIS NOTEBOOKS

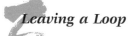

Leaving a Loop

> *Two thousand miles from home, I open a drawer*
> *and—I'd have sworn it was mine,*
> *the weaving lumpy, my fingers*
> *still all thumbs but they loved the peaceful*
> *push pull, pushpull*

The five Robert Frost epigraphs in this book are taken from Robert Frost, *Poetry and Prose*, edited by Edward Connery Lathem and Lawrance Thompson (New York: Holt, Rinehart and Winston, 1972).

so much that one summer
on the boathouse porch with the tree growing
right up through the floor
I made thirty-two
pot holders on the square-jawed metal loom,
stretching colors soft as old rags
soft as this pale buttercup
this faded-eye blue, and the green
fresh as light on maple wings,
seedlight. I wasn't making gifts,
it was the rhythm of the thing
and the small loom, square and safe,
like the four lines of a child's house.
I was homesick,
this was spiderwork, nestwork, easy
till you reached the part where
you unhooked your web from the frame.
Here, see the braided corners, on the last one
somehow you pulled the right thing through
to leave a loop for hanging.
I didn't know I was making gifts
but last winter when my mother died
she still had two, there were stains
and a burn mark, I never thought
of someone's hand feeling
heat through the weave.

Here is a poem neither your students nor mine have ever seen before. I wrote it last night, so it's about as contemporary as you can get, short of sitting down right now and writing your own. To me it's a living, breathing organism—not set in stone; tomorrow I could change it. An organism made of words, that each reader will bring to life in her own way. Emily Dickinson says, "A word is dead/When it is said,/ Some say./ I say it just/ Begins to live/That day."[1]

Whatever my poem means to me, I couldn't possibly reduce this meaning to a prose paraphrase. I don't want to say, "It's about making pot holders when I was young and homesick at summer camp," or "It's really about my loss of my mother," or "Actually it's about applied art versus fine art." Or "It's about the nature of home and separation." I didn't set out, at least consciously, to make a poem about any of this; I wanted to find out why seeing the pot holder when I opened a drawer gave me a sudden, inexplicable urge to write. Now that the poem's written, and I've discovered some answers, I suppose I can say it's about all these things.

But I'm much more interested in asking, "What does it say to you?"—you who are reading it, remember, as if your life depended on it, letting in your beliefs, your dreamlife, your physical sensations—and, I'd add to Adrienne Rich's list, your memories and the mood you happen to be in just now . . . ?

We don't have to start off with a discussion of what poetry is, or with a list of figures of speech, or an argument about whether this is a great poem or a lesser poem. I offer it, you take it or leave it. One thing I try to remember to tell students when the first poem of the year surfaces is that they'll like some poems better than others, regardless of alleged "greatness." I tell them I'm really eager to see which poems each person chooses to talk about during the year ahead—or chooses to read aloud, copy into a notebook, go find more poems by the author of, write a poem back to, or steal words from.

These are all fine responses to a poem, just as good as writing a three-page critical analysis of it. Of course, many college professors won't feel this way, but carpe diem. Right now it's high school. Or junior high. And surely there is life *after* college—some sixty years of it.

There are certain advantages to starting off with a contemporary poem. Fewer footnotes, most likely, which means fewer opportunities for us to display our expertise: "In Shakespeare's day the word 'die' also referred to the moment of sexual consummation. So that's a pun right there. And *there's* an allusion—an indirect reference to religiomythicopastoralhistorical."

Fewer preliminaries, too. Before I hand out Shakespeare's sonnet about envying this man's art and that man's wealth, I may want to do some free-writing with my class on what they most envy in their friends and enemies, perhaps how envy feels, and what they themselves possess that others might envy. This helps create a familiar context for the poem, so that the unfamiliar language and inverted word order won't bring fifteen-year-olds to a grinding halt. Then I'd read it aloud—again, before they see it on the page in all its footnoted and eternal greatness. I might even memorize the poem so I could present it with the conviction and urgency that eye contact can give.

Another reason to start off with some current poems is that the contemporary poet is less prone to view a poem as an opportunity to do some overt teaching: "They also serve who only stand and wait." "The proper study of mankind is man." Teenagers get enough of that from their parents and from us, so it's not surprising if they prefer poems that give them a little more leeway—that let them burrow (or skim) to see what the poem has to offer *them,* not Mankind.

Finally, because a contemporary poem is most apt to be a free-verse personal lyric, expressed in familiar language and syntax, it offers the reader, student and teacher alike, an immediate invitation to "look in thy heart and write." Most of us are not about to try to emulate Keats, Yeats, or Wallace Stevens, much as we may admire them. Sharon Olds, Nikki Giovanni, Quincy Troupe? Maybe.

"Leaving a Loop" actually began with my discovery of a woven pot holder in the drawer of the studio where I'm now writing. There is a little shiver that I think most writers feel when we sense that a poem will happen soon—that a pebble has been cast into the pond. If I can, I sit down right away with a pencil and try to feel where the ripples want me to go. If it happens to me when I've gone for a run, I start trying out lines aloud and memorizing them one by one, as if coiling a rope with no visible end. Since I can't see the end, I try to censor nothing—even if a line or image or word makes no logical sense to me at the time. I let past, present, and future run together, all parts of the braid. I try to leave room for the reader: See? Look here! Just trace this with your finger, feel how loose the weave is? And I try to be absolutely honest, no matter how embarrassing the detail is that's suddenly appeared on the page or how uncomfortable the emotion that's surfaced, or how unanswerable the question.

Later, as the shiver goes away—but never entirely, because revisiting the poem can revive it—I'll listen to the tone and the music, and then rethink the line breaks, maybe consider whether to use stanzas. Where do the reader and I need more air, more pause to think and feel? Where does the emotional shift seem to require a rhythmic shift as well? It's sometimes very hard to hear the tone of one's own poem, especially in the first draft. Will the reader, that mysterious Other, hear what I do? Is this adjective misleading? Is it a false note in the poem's imagery or music?

As I wrote, I was under the spell of the pot holder itself—its sudden appearance, the memories it evoked, the mysterious feel of the twilit studio where I'd be writing for three weeks and the accompanying mystery: why did finding this square of soft colors and rags feel so promising? Why was I so profoundly stirred? It was physical; my eyes were blurry with tears, my hands were shaking. Yet I felt hopeful—almost a spiritual faith that something was about to be revealed.

One kind of reading that I invite students to do, especially with a contemporary poem, is to make a list of questions they'd like to ask the author. If he or she is a fellow student or the teacher or a visiting poet, or if there's a taped interview available, the students may get answers. But a class can also move deep into a poem simply by entertaining one another's questions.

What might you ask about "Leaving a Loop"?

Writing and reading feed each other. When we start writing our own poems, we become much more aware of Dickinson's or Blake's miraculous compression of meaning through image, much more curious (accepting, even) of William Carlos Williams's line breaks. As we read Whitman or Ginsberg, we may realize that our own poems are shutting out rather a lot of the known world. So, engaging with my poem may lead you to your poetry shelves or into writing a poem of your own.

Yes, the odd line break between "thirty-two" and "pot holders" was deliberate, because I wanted to convey the child's pride (and obsession—she kept count) and also to dramatize the word "pot holder," which I'd semiconsciously held off till this late in the poem. Yes, the line near the end, "I didn't know I was making a gift," was a conscious echo of the line up near the middle, "I wasn't making gifts." But I hadn't *planned* the echo; I accepted the idea the moment it hit me—"Oh, yes, that feels right. It corrects, it expands, the earlier line. How interesting." One advantage of having students write poetry is that they are then much less apt to commit the "intentional fallacy"—to assume, for instance, that Frost *intended* "sleep" to symbolize "death" in the line "miles to go before I sleep." The possibility is there in the complex weave of the poet's conscious and unconscious choices—for those readers whose predilections lead them to it. Student poets discover this weave for themselves if we ask them to talk or write about their own poetry-writing process.

Yes, the long, run-on opening sentence of the poem was intentional—in the sense that as I wrote it I was beginning to realize this was a blurry, dreamy, pushpull kind of poem that was pursuing an unknown end and therefore shouldn't have much punctuation. And the last sentence—even

though by then the web has been unhooked from the loom—is also a deliberate run-on because I'm still feeling my way to the discovery about heat,
which in the actual writing didn't occur till the very last line; in the previous two lines I was still rippling outward, or inward, noticing, remembering,
wondering.

As a teenager I used to wait patiently for the muse to descend. But I
don't have time now—and neither do you. I try to engage her (him?) early
in the morning when I'm still barely awake and the night's images—visual
and verbal—are surfacing. Or at night when I'm drowsy but not yet coma-
tose. Poets, like athletes or musicians, need to practice regularly, so that
when the inspiration and opportunity present themselves to make a perfect
pass or give a memorable performance, they'll be ready. I try to write and/
or read poetry every day.

Students can be told, firmly, that yes, there will be moments of inspiration, but for now—there are assignments. Which they may twist somewhat
to their own urgencies, and which may or may not turn out to be poems
they love and want to keep forever. I always add that I'll be happy—even
eager—to read any poems they write on their own. But tonight their assignment is to try writing rhythmic phrases and vivid images to whatever music
they especially love.

Next day, after we listen to these phrases and talk about what it was like
to write to music, I'll give them their first actual poetry-writing assignment:
"Write a poem about getting into someone else's dream. Put us in that
dream. And contrast it in very specific images to your own dreams or
nightmares."

Here's my own "wrong dream" poem, which I recently used as a jumping off point for this assignment. In creating and trying out the exercise, I
discovered that it's important to give students time in class to jot down at
least one dream of their own—in prose, maybe a stream-of-consciousness
prose—and let them read a couple of classmates' dreams, before they start
writing the poem. (Watch out! If you once let them start retelling dreams
aloud, it's impossible to stem the tide!)

It also helps to get them thinking about words. As a warm-up, ask them
to list words they love the sound of. Words they hate the sounds of. And
some colorful variations on a neutral verb like *run* or a common noun like
*house (cave, hacienda, cocoon, airport, chateau, igloo, garbage bin, temple, row
house, cell, tarpaper shack, Sheol, plantation, cabin, adobe, camp, ant hill,*

monastery, soddie, burrow, nest, pond, tent, heart, mind, vein, shoe, trailer, etc.).
Do make time for them to share these words aloud. We all need to be reminded that poems are made of words, and that language, with its mix of
indigenous words, colonialisms, immigrant additions, regional dialects,
coinages, slang or argot, and jargon of all kinds, is a remarkably gorgeous
hodgepodge. Dreams may be blurry, but it takes rich and precise language
to convey your own, unique blur.

Lost

It's tawdry, and there's way too much
noise. I never dream of freaks,
midways, junk food,
and who's the skin-tight mother, jumbo
rollers, she's squealing and flaps
a damp condom at me from the bumper cars
I don't want to meet
this dream's owner, some overgrown
boy I never would have dated
but here he comes singing to me across a crowded
room and I'm soulful, in white,
eyes dilating, he and my mother
the squealer take a shine to each other
she shows him my baby
pictures, oh God not
that one, get me back into
trees and ponds and nocturnes or at least
the one where I can't find my
room and end up teaching math
in a foreign tongue to the whole
football team and it's business
school and nobody but me knows
stream of consciousness
and anyway they're all
asleep

I had a lot of fun writing this—though I admit to censoring the condoms when I read it to freshmen.

Now, try writing your own "wrong dream" poem. Find a space and a chair where you're comfortable. Near a window? In a corner? Outdoors? Do you have a favorite notebook? One where you can copy down lines of poems you like, songs, graffiti, the odd fact, the catchy, overheard turn of phrase, the ambivalent headline, bits of news, jokes, dreams, and recipes? Where you can stash snapshots, leaves, clippings? If it's a brand new notebook, don't be afraid of sullying that first white page with a first effort. My own notebooks are full of first drafts that nobody is going to see. Fill the first page with doodles, if that feels better, and go on to the second. Do you find inspiration at the computer? I need the physical connection of pencil to hand to the rest of me; the computer suits me fine for revising. But some poets start right off on the screen.

Leave yourself at least an hour. The kids will have had class time as well as homework time, remember. Do the warm-ups they're doing. Read your dream and your word lists aloud. Yes, *aloud*. This is important to tell the class as well. Some of your rhythms and mouthmusings may start spinning a poem before you even know what's happening. Close your eyes for a few minutes. Drift . . .

All right, time's up. Tomorrow when you go around the circle or up and down the rows, asking each student to read a couple of favorite lines or to write them up on the wall on the colored mural paper with a magic marker, you'll have some lines to share, too. You may be very proud of them, or you may feel that they pale beside those of your most promising student poets. I find the latter discovery both humbling and inspiring, though which sensation dominates depends on how the day's been going! You'll be curious to compare notes with them about the experience of writing the poem. And because you aren't the expert now but the students' professional colleague, you'll probably pick up a lot of interesting insights into the nature of writing poetry during this discussion.

You may also gain some insights into your students. Here's a "wrong dream" poem by one of the girls in my freshman class. More than anything she'd said or written all first term, this poem helped me understand the brusque, sardonic, boastful person I'd been trying to like. When she read it to the class, it left them totally silent—a real achievement with this group! I took the opportunity to point out that silence can be a tribute, an indication

to a writer that she's moved or challenged her listeners in a really significant way. Several students nodded. "Not every poem has to be discussed,
either," I said. "Some just percolate through your mind for the rest of the
day."

 dream

> this isn't my dream
> i don't move like this
> i don't walk this way
> and these aren't my clothes
> this is my body, but i'm not in control here
> i'm saying something to this boy who
> seems familiar
> suddenly i can see myself
> as if reflected in the water,
> under a dock
> whosever dream this is
> has idealized me
> i'm not this pretty
> i don't stand with this grace
> my hair is more frizzy
> and never stays in beautiful ringlets
>
> whosever dream this is
> has certainly never seen MY hands
> because these
> have fingers
> too long and perfect
> with clean even nails
> and most of all this isn't me because
> whosever dream this is
> loves me for myself
> My own dreams are odd
> and generally
> i'm not allowed to see myself
> because i already know what i'll see

some dreadful caricature
weighing a hundred pounds more
than even i do
with short staticky hair
my grandmother
's nose
no this isn't my dream
i'm beautiful here.

As a result of this assignment, you and your fellow poets may decide to start keeping dream journals. Or you may decide to go in search of other dream poems. Maybe you'll turn up Coleridge's "Kubla Khan." Or Blake's "Chimney Sweep," with the boys locked up in coffins of black and the angel who unlocks them with a golden key. Or my all-time favorite love poem, Margaret Atwood's "Variation on the Word *Sleep*"— "I would like to give you the silver / branch, the small white flower, the one / word that will protect you / from the grief at the center / of your dream. . . ."[2]

Or maybe that most haunting of villanelles, Theodore Roethke's "The Waking": "I wake to sleep, and take my waking slow. / I learn by going where I have to go."[3]

Notes

1. Emily Dickinson, *The Complete Poems,* ed. Thomas H. Johnson (New York: Little, Brown and Co., 1960) 534–535.

2. Margaret Atwood, *Selected Poems II: Poems Selected and New 1976–1986* (Boston: Houghton Mifflin Co., 1987) 77. Both volumes contain poems in a wide range of voices, including mythological women, animals, and a Canadian pioneer woman, and so offer fine examples for students writing persona poems. The poems are also inspiring for young feminists and serious young women writers. Students who already know Atwood as a novelist or know the movie of *The Handmaid's Tale* may be curious about her poems.

3. Theodore Roethke, *The Collected Poems* (New York: Doubleday/Anchor Books, 1975) 104. Roethke's memorable music, his close, tender, witty observation of plants and animals and his haunting poems about the father/son relationship are important to share with students. And with a little help, the sexiness of "I Knew a Woman" can become dazzlingly accessible.

Chapter 3

"Vessel of the Self"

IF LIFE AND THE SOUL ARE SACRED THE HUMAN BODY IS SACRED.

WALT WHITMAN, *"I SING THE BODY ELECTRIC"*

You've already broken down some major barriers. You've written a poem and shared it with your class; you've had a discussion of the poetic process; a sense of community is starting to grow, as the students hear one another's best and worst dreams and the lines they're most proud of having written; perhaps some vivid words and images are going up on the wall and into notebooks. Out of all this you may have already come up with your next assignment. But sooner or later—say, tomorrow—as someone is reading a poem aloud, you notice a pair of glazed eyes in the back row. Frustration kicks in: "He's only here in body."

If he were *fully* here in body, his senses and nerve endings taking in the poem in all its imagery and music and passion, we'd have much to be grateful for! Emotions make themselves felt through the body. And so, therefore, does poetry. A senior girl, looking back to the summer when she was six, described that time almost entirely in terms of motion:

The Half-Dance Afternoon

> Our black baked bodies
> dizzy and loose,
> slick from cheap
> perfume beads half
> danced, dripping in
> a four o'clock summer
> sweat. My boy
> cousins snap their red
> caps, shift their sticky
> squishy tushies
> side to side, inside
> red, hiked, tight
> shorts—still in from '76.
> Our clumpsy, heavy
> dance, pounding the floor
> planks, swaying shoulders
> unsure, my flat six-
> year-old hips
> offbeat to our pretend
> rhythm of the room,
> the salt sting
> wet on tickle-pink lips
> we stayed that summer
> silly, funniness fun
> that afternoon in the room
> where we jiggled and giggled.
> That afternoon we liked
> our being young.

But we tend to subordinate the body to the mind, even though, as psychologist Howard Gardner notes, the body is "the vessel of the individual's sense of self, his most powerful feelings and aspirations."[1]

Can you remember your first awareness of having a body—of breathing, crying, teething, crawling, of noticing your fingers and toes?

Eight o'clock Monday morning: I enter a second-grade art class and read aloud Jacques Prevert's poem, "How to Paint the Portrait of a Bird."[2] Prevert says to paint a cage with the door open and a tree for the bird to sit on, then wait behind the tree for the bird to come. If the painting is good, the bird will sing. The children seize materials and begin drawing or painting their bird. Soon they dance up, sashay or strut, thrusting the picture at me and demanding, "Does it sing?" Tuesday, 10:00 a.m.: In another second-grade class I broach the question, "What could you hear if you had magic ears? Close your eyes and don't talk, just listen." Heads go down on desks, fingers press over eyes, bodies quiver with badly suppressed giggles. Then a hand shoots up. "I'd hear ants dance." And her hips sway in the chair, her shoulders wiggle. She is a dancing ant.

But when I do breathing exercises with eighth and ninth graders, I notice how self-conscious they are. Even with eyes closed there are worries: Do I look funny doing this? Are my breasts sticking out? Am I having an erection? Do I look fat? Am I breathing louder than anybody else?

Since poetry can speak so powerfully to our bodies—even de-glaze our eyes—it's important to help students become more comfortable with their physical selves. With greater awareness of sensation—heaviness, lightness, tension, contraction, release, softness, abrasiveness—will come a heightened access to one's emotions. And to poetry.

Early in the year, but not until the class and I have begun to know one another, I bring in a small packet of "body poems"—William Carlos Williams's "Smell!",[3] Lucille Clifton's poems on her hips and her hair,[4] Langston Hughes's "Dream Variations,"[5] Ruth Stone's "Message from Your Toes"[6] (a bizarre love poem focusing on her dead husband's broken toe), Nikki Giovanni's "Ego Tripping,"[7] and some poems by former students. It's good to have a range of races, genders, and ages represented in the packet. We share the poems aloud, commenting on how images and sounds and shapes convey the poets' attitudes toward their bodies. In discussing *attitude*, we're really discussing *tone*, though we may not use this term yet.

To help physicalize the words on the page, I get the students doing jumping jacks or tightening and then relaxing every muscle—clenching teeth and fists, squinting, drawing up their knees to their chests, and finally, holding their breaths. They become aware of how different "tense" feels from "loose."

Then I ask them to close their eyes and choose one part of their body that they like or that intrigues them—nails, hands, eyes, belly button, hair, hips—and just think about why they like it—even make up boasts about it, even downright lies. I remind them of Giovanni's "Ego Tripping," a wild, flamboyant boast about how great she is, what powers the various parts of her body have—"I . . . blew / My nose, giving oil to the arab world," "My bowels deliver uranium." I remind them of Clifton's poem to her hips:

> these hips are magic hips.
> i have known them
> to put a spell on a man and
> spin him like a top!

Then we all write boasts about our bodies. This is very hard for some of us! But the more self-consciousness and shame one comes to feel about one's body, the harder it is to hear what it has to say about feelings. Perhaps the household you grew up in wasn't so different from mine? There was little physical contact between my parents, my four siblings, and me, other than the hug after a prolonged absence. I agonized about my appearance, especially in a leotard, and was allowed to assume that the ideal girl looked like Sandra Dee on the cover of *American Girl Magazine*. (At least it wasn't Kate Moss.) I hated buying and wearing bathing suits, shorts, jeans, all the revealing paraphernalia of summer camp. I envied the confident, high-kicking girls on the cheerleading squad, even while feeling intense scorn for this activity. At home, the mind was what mattered. We weren't encouraged to think about physical pleasure. Sitting in the sun was a waste of time unless you were reading a book or mending a shirt, and sex wasn't discussed. But alone in the woods by the lake near our Maine cabin or in the overgrown tangle of berry bushes and wildflowers behind our house in Connecticut, my senses opened. My body relaxed, as it forgot the urgent need to make itself as small and thin and unobtrusive as possible, and I reveled in smells and sounds, the sun on my skin, and the presence of something I was later to learn about from Wordsworth and Hopkins—"the sense sublime / Of something far more deeply interfused,"[8] "the dearest freshness deep down things."[9] What poetry I wrote in those years sprang from such moments—and from the poignant sensuousness of music. I feel tremendous gratitude toward my parents for making the beauty of music and nature available. But as I look back on that time, I feel like a child put out to run free in a flowery meadow, blindfolded, gagged, and leashed.

I empathized with the self-consciousness of my ninth graders. But by the next day, when we shared our poems, it was clear that the free, celebratory spirit and quirky wit of the packet poems had been contagious. I could almost feel bodies—and imaginations—expanding. Ari, an athlete afflicted with the name Ariadne and not normally given to poetry, had played with some of the questions I'd put on the board the day before. *To what could you compare this part of your body? What good is it? What sort of art would it make? How would you trace its history, from birth to death?*

Ode to My Button

> *O my bellybutton: How I salute you.*
> *You with your precocious flaps of skin,*
> > *A shrivelled, wrinkled raisin,*
> *A canyon, a dangerous break in the smooth belly skin.*
> *Possibly a pitfall for a wandering ant.*
> *You are simply a confused, inside-out umbilical cord.*
> > *Serving no purpose, really.*
> > *But you are there,*
> *One of my most prized possessions.*
> *A piece of art stuck to a barren desert floor.*
> > *Once a most vital organ,*
> > *Supplying life to a seedling,*
> *Now you just collect lint.*

Another girl assumed the voice of her leg, and confronted her worries about its ugliness:

> *Why do so many people think I'm fat?*
> *I must have many powerful muscles in me.*
> *Just think if you didn't have muscle around your*
> *Femur, Tibia, and Fibula,*
> *they could rot away.*
> *Stop insulting me!*

Brandi, a lively, confident girl who clearly identified with both Giovanni's and Clifton's voices, praised her skin:

> I am a black woman,
> A black woman I am proud to be.
>
> With every bite of creamy, imperial chocolate you eat,
> I want you to remember that it's my brown, smooth skin
> you taste.
> . . . .
> My sleek, shapely body
> Gave the coca-cola bottle and hourglass their shape.
> It was my gorgeous legs
> Which put the leg in elegant, and gave it
> its true meaning.

And Pearl expressed similar pride:

> You call them slanted
> But to me they're almond shaped.
> My eyes are special eyes.
> They can see what others can't.
> They separate me from everyone else
> and force me to look back to where I came from.
> It is a symbol of Asians
> that is never missed.
> These eyes are special eyes.

You may find, as I often do with this exercise, that the boys seem more interested than the girls in pursuing witty or surreal analogies and less comfortable with "owning" or taking sensuous pleasure in their bodies. For example, Zack, one of my freshmen, wrote:

> I would cut off my lips.
> Leave them wriggling at my feet,
> Bloody on white tiles,

Fat, red, pointless worms.
begging to be pasted back on,
burrowing into the ground.
A man orders a man to be shot.
A couple kisses.
It is all done with lips
I watch my lips in the mirror.
A gaping hole into myself
opens, for any creature to jump into.
For any lie to twist out of.
I will knot my throat shut.
I will reveal nothing. . . .

As the boys grow to manhood, I worry that they'll lose the playfulness apparent in Zack's poem and retain only the distrust. That they'll pay attention to the body only when it makes demands on them in sex or sports—or when it betrays them. And what about the girls? Every year now I'm more aware of anorexia among them. Some of the junior and senior girls write anxious poems about anorexic friends. A few even write about themselves. Though these poems are troubling, at least they bring the issue into the open and can lead to helpful discussion, even to intervention.

At the very least, this assignment is usually an occasion for humor and pride, for lively language and a greater appreciation of the value of the concrete and the sensuous in poetry. From here it's a natural step to *reading* poems with your body. Then the silent page becomes once again the living organism that grew from a poet's shiver.

Notes

1. Howard Gardner, *Frames of Mind: The Theory of Multiple Intelligences* (New York: Basic Books, 1983) 235. Gardner's theory that each learner has a dominant kind of "intelligence" through which she learns most readily (though she is capable of "knowing the world" through all seven)—not merely linguistic and logical-mathematical but spatial, musical, bodily-kinesthetic, interpersonal, and intrapersonal—suggests the potential richness of poetry's appeal, and the importance of making it accessible in ways that tap into all of these learning styles. At several different points in the school year, I ask each

of my students to check off which ones of these seven they feel most attuned to—what kinds of learners they sense that they might be—and we discuss as a class the value of having so many different kinds of strengths available among our classmates. But I also file away these checklists to consult whenever I have a bad day with a particular class or student; they sometimes provide useful clues.

2. Jacques Prevert in *Voices in the Gallery: Poems & Pictures Chosen by Dannie and Joan Abse* (London: Tate Gallery Publications, 1986) 166. This is a very beautiful book, with reproductions of paintings and sculptures that range from Brueghel and Uccello and Michelangelo to the Impressionists, Klimt, Picasso, Duchamp, Rothko, Bacon, and Giacometti. Each artwork is paired with a poem. Prevert's poem is opposite Braque's *School Prints—'The Bird,'* a charming, playful, childlike piece; one can easily see how it could have inspired Prevert's poem. I've also used with success Giacometti's *Dog* and Robert Wallace's poem about that sculpture. We look at the visual piece, generate word lists and create voices for the figures or objects or shapes and colors, and write for a while. Then we share our pieces and listen to the voice from the book. We may steal some of the poet's words and techniques for our poetry journals. Another book that combines beautiful reproductions with poems is *Talking to the Sun: An Illustrated Anthology of Poems for Young People*, selected and introduced by Kenneth Koch and Kate Farrell (New York: The Metropolitan Museum of Art/Henry Holt and Company, 1985). Every school library should have both these books!

3. William Carlos Williams, *Collected Poems,* ed. Christopher McGowan and Walton Litz, vol. 1 (New York: New Directions, 1988) 92.

4. Lucille Clifton, *homage to my hair, homage to my hips, good woman: poems and a memoir 1969–1980* (Brockport NY: BOA Editions, Ltd., 1987) 167–168. A powerful African American voice that in its clarity and spareness, its anger and tenderness, knows, as Clifton has said, that we write poems to discover the questions, not to find answers.

5. Langston Hughes, *The Collected Poems,* ed. Arnold Rampersad (New York: Random House/Vintage, 1995) 40. Most high schoolers have encountered a few of Hughes's poems as children, or in junior high, so to "make it new," you may want to approach Hughes as a blues poet. *Literary Cavalcade*, a very useful magazine on high school writing, which your school library may carry, regularly features a different poet with accompanying exercises, and one of

their back issues has a good presentation of Hughes as a blues poet. You can find a good definition of the blues as a poetic form in Ron Padgett's *Handbook of Poetic Forms* (New York: Teachers and Writers Collaborative, 1987).

6. Ruth Stone, *Second-Hand Coat* (Boston: David R. Godine, 1987) 25. Stone's language is fresh, unpredictable, and feisty in its chronicling of the tragicomic nature of love, aging, illness, and politics. Some Jewish students may hear, especially in her later poems, the voice of their own grandmothers.

7. Nikki Giovanni, *Selected Poems* (New York: William Morrow, 1996) 92–93. Students can fall in love with Giovanni's poetry in their childhood, for she has seven very appealing collections for children—*Spin a Soft Black Song,* for example—and will go on reading her through junior high and high school. Some of my students have enjoyed grappling with the issues in her essay collection, *Racism 101.*

8. William Wordsworth, "Lines Composed a Few Miles above Tintern Abbey on Revisiting the Banks of the Wye During a Tour, July 13, 1798," *Selected Poetry*, ed. Mark Van Doren (New York: Random House, 1950) 106. The classic "memory poem," this can be most easily read, I think, *after* students have already written poems of their own about revisiting a favorite place. It makes a rather daunting model, but becomes more meaningful, more worth the struggle, the more a student can bring his own experience to bear on it.

9. Gerard Manley Hopkins, "God's Grandeur," *Poems of Gerard Manley Hopkins* (London: Oxford University Press, 1948) 70. Hopkins has been called "the poet's poet," which can sound like the kiss of death to a student, but he's a great example of poetic license and his gloriously compounded words—"fresh-firecoal chestnut-falls," "silk-sack clouds," "very-violet-sweet," "bone-house," "dare-gale skylark"— can inspire students to create their own. Kenneth Koch and Kate Farrell in *Sleeping on the Wing* (New York: Vintage, 1982) offer a nice clutch of Hopkins lyrics followed by a good writing assignment.

Chapter 4

"Written on the Body"—Reading the Poem

THE BEST READER OF ALL IS ONE WHO WILL READ, CAN READ, NO FASTER THAN HE CAN HEAR THE LINES AND SENTENCES IN HIS MIND'S EAR AS IF ALOUD. FREQUENTING POETRY HAS SLOWED HIM DOWN BY ITS METRIC OR MEASURED PACE.

ROBERT FROST, FROM HIS NOTEBOOKS

By now perhaps your students are starting to collect poems by their peers, poems from packets you've given them, poems from anthologies you've brought into class. On the other hand—perhaps they haven't yet caught fire. They may like writing their own poems but have little patience with the Norton Anthology or *Sound and Sense* or the poetry in their American Literature text. They need help in order to actually hear and heft and feel the printed poem.

Ideally, the words should come alive in a rush of smells, textures, sounds, and tastes. But regaining the power to read this creatively, a birthright which most of us lost somewhere in elementary school, all too soon after learning to read, is akin to mastering a second language. The thrill of reading a poem with the body is like the connection that burst on Helen Keller when she felt the water gush over her hand and suddenly realized it was the equivalent of the word WATER, that her teacher Anne Sullivan had spelled into her hand so many times. For us, this experience is reversed. We can read *water* with our brain, but we can't feel the stream gush over our fingers as we do so.

It's hard to challenge students' assumption that, after ten years of practice, they know how to read. So start with skills they're less confident about. Memorizing and reciting a poem can get it off the page and into the bloodstream. The attention one must give to rhythm, rhyme, and other patterns in order to learn the piece by heart and communicate it leads to a very physical encounter with the words and emotions. But I find memorization difficult myself, and I know from experience that unless we make time to give students help with the process, they can simply end up associating poetry with frustration and failure.

A poem does become more fully yours when your body moves with it. I once witnessed poet/teacher Georgia Heard recite Langston Hughes's "My People" [1] from memory, using her body as well as her voice:

The night is beautiful,   [Look up, lift arms, spread them
                                     outward]
So the faces of my people.   [Touch face]

The stars are beautiful,   [Look up, lift arms, close and
                                     open fingers repeatedly]
So the eyes of my people.   [Touch eyes with fingertips]

Beautiful, also, is the sun.   [Extend arms together at one
                                     side of body and sweep them up
                                     and around in a half circle]
Beautiful, also, are the souls of my people.
                                     [Move hand to heart]

Trying out these moves with young children, I found they helped us memorize the poem and say it together. A number of first graders went home that night and recited it to their parents, complete with gestures. It also made me more aware of the dynamic of the poem—the way Hughes's spirit seems to expand as his vision of blackness embraces the beauty of the heavens. Repeatedly, the body is invited to move outward and inward, systole, diastole, capturing the emotional rhythms of the poem and helping the reader feel Hughes's spirit move toward a vision of blackness that can challenge the constricting forces of prejudice and shame.

But older students tend to be self-conscious about "performing" a lyric poem with gestures; it feels childish. So it works better to start them off reciting poetic drama, where "acting" seems more necessary and natural. I ask my high schoolers to choose a favorite speech from whatever Shakespeare play we're studying. No matter how much we've discussed its imagery and sound, they're invariably startled to realize that a play might "count" as poetry. This is a good occasion to point out that poetry can be dramatic or narrative as well as lyric, and to offer them examples of dramatic monologues—even try writing some.

I make a big deal out of this recitation project, because it does lead the class to understand the difference between the lines on the page and the poetry felt in their bodies and, consequently, understood in their hearts. We spend a week making notes, exploring subtext, rehearsing, and finally, performing.

First I read at least one soliloquy aloud to the class in a variety of ways, asking for reactions. I ask them to pick out the lines that strike them as most powerful, most memorable, most significant, and to consider what they suggest about the speaker—why that particular metaphor, that image, that pattern of harsh, explosive syllables. I ask to what degree the speech feels private or public—and how my voice and breathing and eyes could make us feel this. I demonstrate some possibilities of movement—turning my back on the audience, putting myself at a higher elevation, lowering my eyes, tensing or loosening my body. And I offer a few "don'ts": Don't pace aimlessly back and forth for the entire speech or sway from one foot to another with military precision. (Though all rules are made to be broken; perhaps the situation and language ask the reader to pace or sway.)

Jay, a freshman, has chosen one of Iago's monologues. She reads her speech over aloud at home a number of times, making notes and looking up any words she's unsure of. In class she works on enunciation, breathing, volume, and pace, first by herself and then with a partner to "coach" her. The next night she is to mark the "beats"—not the meter, but the actor's "beats," the shifts in thought or mood or tone that occur, her shifts in intent. What clues do images and sound patterns offer to the poem's subtext, to the speaker's fear or desire or need? In class she and her partner explore the intonations and physical movements that feel most natural and that best communicate the subtext. I notice that her need to move around and make eye contact leads her to want to let go of the book; and kinesthetic or muscle memory helps her master the words by associating them with the learned movements.

Two days later she's off book and performs the speech for the class. I'm impressed by her decision to address most of the lines to a knife she has brought in as her prop. In her notes she explains: "This is a soliloquy—it's private, so I won't look at the audience, except maybe right at the end, when Iago wants people to know how clever he is. His mind is sharp and mean, like a knife. He's a villain. Later he causes a lot of deaths. He likes risks. He likes feeling the edge and point of the knife. He likes it even better than money." As I watch and listen to Jay's performance and later as I read these notes, I'm satisfied that the poetry is lodged now in her bones and heart as well as her mind.

How can we transfer this physicality to the process of reading a *lyric* poem? Take Wordsworth's sonnet "The World Is Too Much with Us," which we can find in almost any anthology of great poems in English.[2] To some students these fourteen lines on the page might as well be cuneiform. There's no necessity for acting it out. But receiving any poem's energy and responding to it has to be a physical act as well as a mental one.

> The world is too much with us; late and soon,
> Getting and spending, we lay waste our powers:
> Little we see in Nature that is ours;
> We have given our hearts away, a sordid boon!
> This Sea that bares her bosom to the moon;
> The winds that will be howling at all hours,
> And are up-gathered now like sleeping flowers;
> For this, for everything, we are out of tune;
> It moves us not.—Great God! I'd rather be
> A Pagan suckled in a creed outworn;

So might I, standing on this pleasant lea,
Have glimpses that would make me less forlorn;
Have sight of Proteus rising from the sea;
Or hear old Triton blow his wreathèd horn.

It's tempting to make a lesson plan on sonnets, or on Romanticism, or to assign an analytical essay or embark on a discussion of materialism and environmental pollution, but don't do any of the above until you've read the poem *aloud*. Take a few deep breaths first, and then read slowly, letting your body respond to the heft and pace of individual lines and phrases. Even if you've read and taught this poem a hundred times before. Feel the music in your mouth. Breathe with the speaker. Take your time. Don't get hung up on the iambic pentameter beat. Poet/teacher John Timpane offers some good advice: "Meter is just an imaginary pattern; you're not supposed to let it straightjacket you. . . . The meter is something a poet sets up in your head, much as a drummer might rap out an intro to a song, to give you the time signature. . . . The difference between meter and rhythm is the difference between the beat of a song and what's actually played over the beat. . . . The poem speaks conversationally over the meter." [3]

Hear the rushed clutter of short syllables in "getting and spending" as opposed to the second half of the line, those strong, damning monosyllables—"we lay waste our powers." That's the rhythm or conversation over the beat. Feel what the two contrasting halves of that line do in your mouth—the teeth and tongue work of the first half and the work with lips and throat and even the chest that the second half requires. How does your breathing change in the second half?

The first line of the poem feels burdensome to me, and when I look and listen more closely, caught up in this sensation, I realize my body must have responded instinctively to the weight of the line's ten successive monosyllables. (I wasn't assigned to scan the meter; my own body has nudged me into curiosity. Teaching scansion can wait.) The two pairs of words, "late and soon," "getting and spending," also weigh me down with their iteration, their accumulation. As the rhythms and sense of the words are making a physical impact on me, they're also having an emotional effect: "lay waste our powers," "Little we see in nature that is ours," and "sordid boon" feel dispiriting, wearying, emptying.

Reaching the fifth line, I feel a contrasting movement of release, outward and upward, as the sea "bares her bosom to the moon" and the howl-

ing winds "are upgathered now like sleeping flowers." But by line 8, the
heaviness and weariness return. I'm responding, I think, initially to the
weight, the accumulating force, of "for this, for everything," and the next
line's terse monosyllables, "It moves us not." For me it feels like trying to
cross a threshold—emotional, perhaps sexual—and being flung back. Or like
trying to lift myself out of depression and falling back into it.

The last six lines do lift me up and outward again, starting with the
speaker's exclamation, "Great God!"—which feels like both prayer and curse,
an emotional release like that of suddenly being able to cry, the throat and
chest loosening, opening up. It's related to that physical response I have in
reading "The Rime of the Ancient Mariner," when the albatross falls from
the mariner's neck, a spring of love gushes from his heart, and he's able to
bless the water snakes without thinking about it. This sensation lets me
cross a threshold and enter into Wordsworth's vision at the end of the
sonnet—two lines that again feel like a release, the upward movement of
Proteus rising from the sea and the outward movement of Triton blowing
his horn.

Taken into our bodies, this poem can become immediately, urgently,
our own, engraving itself on muscle and breath, oppressing, constricting,
releasing. Our bodies replicate the two contrasting energies within the
speaker, making the poem more memorable because more fully experienced, more felt.

We have been conditioned to view body and mind as two separate
entities, the first merely a container for the second. And we tend to assume
that aesthetic appreciation of literature is a "purely" intellectual affair.
Patterns of words, colors, movements, are registering all over our bodies,
translating themselves into streams of sensations, while we rush to focus
"mind" on conducting its lofty, impersonal task of abstracting, analyzing,
and judging. Before we ask students to analyze the "meaning" of lines on a
page, we need to help them—and ourselves—learn to pause and feel the
water gush over our fingers as we read or hear the word. This sensation is a
vital part of the *meaning* of "water." Once we have experienced it, we may
really *want* to talk and write about the poetry of water. And we may begin to
see more in nature—and in poetry—that is ours.

If earlier you prepared for writing "body poems" with your class by
actually doing the exercises in tightening parts of the body and then releasing the tension, you might preface their reading of Wordsworth's sonnet—

which *you* have now read "as if your life depended on it"—with a breathing exercise for the students. I like to start this with a few minutes of very strenuous jumping in place, to leave them panting, eager to shut up and sit down. Then, if there's room, ask everyone to sit on the floor, facing away from the people nearest them. Or if this is impossible, let them sit with their heads down on their desks. You might dim the lights and even put on a tape of very quiet music; I often use Native American flute music.

Ask the students to close their eyes and concentrate on their breathing—which should now be tumultuous from all that jumping. See if they can tune out everything else—they might even check their pulse from time to time—and imagine that they're large Chinese jars, or hollow trees, filling and then emptying, inhale, exhale. Nothing matters but their breathing; it's keeping them alive. Its rate is different from anyone else's, but at the same time they're all united by the need to breathe and their present concentration. Suggest that they check their body for tension and try to expel it as they exhale.

When they're focused and quiet, turn off the tape of music, and ask them to listen to you reading "The World Is Too Much with Us." Ask them not to worry about unfamiliar words or allusions but to try breathing quietly with the lines that give them a relaxed or expansive or rising feeling and shift their breathing when a line feels tense or heavy or agitated. Try this several times. Then hand out copies of the poem and ask them to mark the lines according to how they breathed. Discuss. Or if you don't want to break the quiet, ask them to write a bit in their notebooks about what just went on. *Then* discuss.

If they seem interested, try the same approach with a contemporary, free verse poem, maybe Galway Kinnell's "Wait," which he wrote for someone who was contemplating suicide.[4]

> *Wait, for now.*
> *Distrust everything if you have to.*
> *But trust the hours. Haven't they*
> *carried you everywhere, up to now?*
> *Personal events will become interesting again.*
> *Hair will become interesting.*
> *Pain will become interesting.*
> *Buds that open out of season will become interesting.*

Second-hand gloves will become lovely again;
their memories are what give them
the need for other hands. And the desolation
of lovers is the same: that enormous emptiness
carved out of such tiny beings as we are
asks to be filled; the need
for the new love is faithfulness to the old.

Wait.
Don't go too early.
You're tired. But everyone's tired.
But no one is tired enough.
Only wait a little and listen:
music of hair,
music of pain,
music of looms weaving all our loves again.
Be there to hear it, it will be the only time,
most of all to hear
the flute of your whole existence,
rehearsed by the sorrows, play itself into total exhaustion.

Ask several different students to take turns reading this aloud, and again let people mark the lines. I find that discussion of both poems' breathing patterns leads very naturally into further observations on their content and style. Don't worry if students aren't using correct terminology; this is a good opportunity for you to casually slip in some of it—"Yes, poets call that image you liked a metaphor"—and offer, or get them to offer, further examples; make up some together on the board. Learning a literary term before they feel any need for it simply distances them from the literature—makes poetry appear as an arcane discipline, like something not for them. (The way I feel when people use computer jargon about an operation I haven't learned yet.) "Yes, the reason that line feels so heavy to you is the chain of long, open vowels—feel what's going on in your mouth and throat and chest when you say them? Poets call this repetition 'assonance.' Try writing a few lines with some good assonance in your notebook. What sort of feelings do you associate with light, quick vowels—as opposed to those long ones that come from the back of your mouth and throat?"

From these experiences should come a new kind of reading. But it takes reinforcement. Because for so many years we've been processing the printed page simply to find out as efficiently as possible "what happens next" or "what's the point." Fortunately, poems are generally short; if we catch ourselves slipping back into the old, evil ways, we can always start over.

Make some time for silent reading in class prefaced with three minutes of some physical or vocal activity that reminds everyone they are breathing, pulsating organisms with ears and tongues and fingertips and muscles and nerves—not reading machines. Find out early in the year who your artists, dancers, and musicians are, and encourage them to present collages, paintings, choreography, and music in response to specific poems.

Whenever the class shares poems they've written or collected, make sure to ask for some responses to the *physical* sensations created through imagery, sound effects, and movement.

And finally, make lots of analogies—say, to sports and music; how in reading poems, just as in playing basketball or singing, your senses and muscles let you know if you're "doing it right." Suggest that reading a poem the old way is like reading a book on sex instead of making love. Well, all right—say it's like reading recipes all day instead of eating the food.

Notes

1. Hughes, 36 (see note 5, chap. 3).

2. Wordsworth, 536 (see note 8, chap. 3).

3. John Timpane, *It Could Be Verse* (Albany, CA: BOAZ, 1995) 21–22. This is a very funny, very reassuring book, subtitled *Anybody's Guide to Poetry,* by a poet and teacher who demystifies and remystifies poetry. Timpane uses "funky" icons to mark typical questions people are afraid to ask about poetry and then offers direct, practical answers, always turning to a specific poem to help him. Like Rich, he's committed to the idea that poetry makes your life better, and he begins by teaching you how to read it aloud and hear it on the page. The book includes lists and descriptions (with quotes) of sixty-six great poets, ancient and modern, a list of magazines where you can find good poetry, and a glossary of terms.

4. Galway Kinnell, *Selected Poems* (Boston: Houghton Mifflin, 1982) 127. Galway Kinnell's poems speak to your blood and breath and are wonderful for reading aloud. They can help students acknowledge their own fears and joys and losses, and they can inspire an enthusiasm for sensuous language. Try "Blackberry Eating," "After Making Love We Hear Footsteps," "Saint Francis and the Sow," and "First Song"; then perhaps two longer, more mysterious poems, "The Bear" and "Little Sleep's-Head Sprouting Hair in the Moonlight." Students can learn a lot about the power of images from all these poems.

Chapter 5

Writing about Poems—or Putting Off the Analytical Essay

> *HERE AGAIN, PERHAPS I AM OLD-FASHIONED. YOUTH, I BELIEVE, SHOULD NOT ANALYZE ITS ENJOYMENTS. IT SHOULD LIVE. . . . CRITICISM IS THE PROVINCE OF AGE, NOT OF YOUTH. THEY'LL GET TO THAT SOON ENOUGH. LET THEM BUILD UP A FRIENDSHIP WITH THE WRITING WORLD FIRST. ONE CAN'T COMPARE UNTIL ONE KNOWS.*
>
> ROBERT FROST, INTERVIEW WITH ROSE C. FELD

The average student—99 percent of all the students I've ever taught, anyway—honestly can't see why anyone would want to analyze a poem for two or three pages when he could be—well, writing or reading *more* poems. It's plain unnatural. If he doesn't love poetry to start with, it's like being forced to eat, very slowly and at gunpoint, a huge platter of brussels sprouts, then regurgitate them and slowly ingest the limp, steamy, cabbagy little suckers all over again. If he does love poetry, it's like doing the same thing with pizza. Either way, regurgitation and conspicuous lack of immediate gratification.

It's bad enough to write an analysis of *The Scarlet Letter*, but at least there you have hundreds of pages—an intricate plot, a set of complex characters, and controversial issues. It doesn't feel like you're "tearing it apart"—rather, that from a huge forest you're selecting a single tree; lots of other trees will remain untouched. But to get three pages of essay out of one fourteen-line poem is bound to feel like clear cutting.

Then, too, the traditional way of starting a critical analysis of a poem is to define the situation, speaker, and tone. Any student worth her salt is likely to wonder, "Who out there has asked for this information? My teacher already knows. And if it's not obvious from reading the poem—then how am *I* supposed to figure it out? So this is a trap! Either way, I feel kind of dumb."

It's relatively easy to make a student feel you are curious to hear her views on the state of Roger Chillingworth's soul—and to convince her that in order to explore this matter in an essay she'll have to refer to specific moments in the novel. But the essence of a lyric poem does not lie, generally speaking, in its "issues." If we pretend it does, we do the poem a disservice. It doesn't lie in narrative structure or character development. It's a distillation, a concentration, of the sensuous and emotional content of an experience, maybe a moment—made memorable through the poet's intuitive and conscious creation of imagery and music. Of course, there is narrative poetry, but that's not what we tend to ask our students to analyze.

So, given the complex nature of the lyric poem, I wait till the end of junior year to show students how to write the traditional analytical essay, and even then I encourage them to write in the first person. By that point, they've written and revised their own poems, read a wide range of other people's, and are ready to take an interest in how a poem "works." They can begin to articulate what impact the poet's imagery and music have on their own feelings—though even then, and even with students who are very sensitive to these things, finding the language and sentence structure in which to talk about this intricate weave of elements is a major struggle. And only worthwhile to the student if she believes I am genuinely interested in her particular reading of the poem. I can point out, "But overlooking the fact that the abusive father in Komunyakaa's poem can't write really means you haven't yet read the poem the author wrote—so let's take another look." But

I don't think I can say, "It's irrelevant to your essay that your own father is abusive."

So—if you want to lead gently toward writing analytical essays, or even forget about it—we can ask students to write a *letter* to Galway Kinnell containing very specific questions about "Wait", including questions about word choices, line breaks, etc. And then they can write his answer for him.

Or we can simply divide the class into small groups, give each a large sheet of colored paper, and see which group can collect the greatest number of specific observations on this poem—facts, facts, facts, not interpretations. (Why colored paper? It seems to induce a relaxed, playful, vaguely artistic mood that makes them feel nostalgic for their childhood. I guess. Same reason I hand out apples on days when I want them curled up in corners browsing in poetry books. "Pretend you're in an attic, up under the eaves, and it's raining very gently. There's a bird's nest in the big maple just outside the window—you can hear the babies cheeping—and a bunch of old books with faded covers and neat pictures, that your dad read the summer when he was fourteen.")

Get some observations from each group up on the board. This usually makes an impressive array, and students are surprised at how clever they are. (As opposed to how they feel about their analytical essays at this stage of the game.) Then ask them, "You're poets yourselves. You know what it's like to write a poem. So pick one of these observations on the board and tell us why you chose to write the poem this way—with all those long vowels, say? And *did* you choose to do it? Or did it just happen? Or did you notice a few long vowels, feel they were effective, and add a few more?" Turn to someone else and ask, "You've read a lot of poems. How did those long vowels affect you when you read them and listened to them?" Let the two have a brief conversation about this. Or divide the whole class into poets and readers, letting each person choose a couple of observations from the board to account for. The ensuing discussion will probably reveal a surprising amount of agreement as to the effects of specific artistic choices. This inspires the students with confidence in their ability to read a poem; it's not, after all, just a game of Russian roulette. They're analyzing the poem without quite realizing it—not "tearing it apart" but putting it back together for themselves.

Another ploy is to assign an informal journal piece: "Describe in great physical, sensory detail a personal experience in which your body registered emotion." Encourage them to develop a poem from this entry. Some may go straight to the poem, bypassing the prose description. But it's a good way to get into a discussion of differences and similarities between poetry and poetic prose. It's also helpful to those students who love writing description but are terrified of writing literary analysis. Later in the year you can lead them to see a relationship between the two processes by asking them to "describe" a poem.

If you haven't yet tried free association with the class, this is a great time to do it—while they're becoming more aware of poets' techniques and are still excited about writing their own poems. It can lead them to a more subtle understanding of how a poet arrives at the most mysterious parts of her poem, and how reductive paraphrasing a poem can be. There are always some student writers who start out with the conviction that "technique" is a dirty word—that poetry is spontaneous, a trancelike outpouring, and if their poems come out in forced rhymes or in abstract nouns or clichés, that's what the muse delivered; it's their natural voice and shouldn't be tampered with. These poets should feel right at home with free-association and its mystical, streamlike flow! It's harder for the rational and rather literal types who are still writing earnest poems about how to reach the goal by striving; or for the tense perfectionists who want to control the whole process and know where they'll end before they start. However, it's useful for everyone in coping with the wild leaps of association they'll find in many twentieth century poems. (See Robert Bly's book of translations and criticism called *Leaping Poetry*.[1]) It can also lead student poets to fresher language and imagery and some exciting, unexpected moves from one section of a poem to another.

Bring in an alarm clock so you can write along with the class. From a poem you've just read together, choose an important word, one that's evocative, concrete, rich in connotation, perhaps one that can be used as several different parts of speech—a word like *garden, grab, window, knife, wolf, door, cellar* . . . In working with Wordsworth's sonnet, for example, you might choose *spend.* You all write the word at the top of a blank page in your notebooks. Then for four minutes write without thinking—whatever words the pencil chooses, taking off from *spend.* The rules are: no stopping—the pencil must move as fast as possible; it's fine to repeat a word until the pencil's ready to move on; don't try to make sense, or to write sentences or phrases—don't *try* at all. Just keep those words streaming out. When time is up, ask students to circle any associations that interest them—for unexpected meaning, for interesting music, for imagery, or for fresh, startling juxtaposition. Share favorites aloud or on mural paper. Explain that the more they practice this exercise on their own, the more they'll find they can "let go" and gain access to their unconscious—a very important source of inspiration for poets. I often start off free associating in my notebook when I have no idea of what I want to write.

So what did yours look like? The first time you try this in class, you may need to watch them out of the corner of your eye as you write, to prod those who are inclined to stop and think. You may even sacrifice your own creativity in favor of walking around the room to encourage the constant flow of words. But with many classes, the mere sight of their teacher scribbling madly, head bent over the page, will inspire a similar effort.

My own one- or two-minute stream (before I went over to encourage a student whose pencil had apparently suffered a breakdown): *spend rush time smitten with trees love hinge hanging away sloth idol waste spend sex water blood lilies under crystal stalagmite stagnate spend natal mosquito marsh pond stagnate ignite aqueous nitrous oxide explosion plode implode pleiades aide de camp memoir AIDS spend help sacrifice give up give out outhouse entirely outerbanks drift spend trust fund fins fin de siecle spent weary yellow dogged foxed faded fade out blues*

At the very least this brief burst reminded me of some words I have yet to use in a poem. Some day I may start one with the line "Time smitten with trees." Or I could write an essay on spending time—wasting, idling, stagnating, igniting, giving up, giving out, drifting, wearying, yellowing, spending myself in sex, growing downward drip by drip like a stalactite, rushing, putting time in a trust fund, heading for the outer banks, the fin de siecle, setting my time in crystal, toiling not—like the lilies, how fair they are, simply lolling about in the shade smitten with trees . . . And I'm now much more interested in writing an essay about what Wordsworth means by "Getting and spending, we lay waste our powers."

Students tend to write much better when they're allowed to choose from a variety of topics or forms. You might invite the class to write in response to Wordsworth's sonnet: a poem of their own, a personal essay about what a line or theme or image in the poem means to them, a letter to the poet and his answer back, a description of different ways in which the poem registered on them (on their body, their feelings, their mind?), or a comparison to Kinnell's poem. You could ask that they incorporate some of Wordsworth's language into whatever they write, in one way or another. And if you give them a rubric—a list of goals for which you'll hold everyone accountable when you assess the work, you can make certain that whatever form or approach they choose they'll have to: (a) present the work in two different stages of progress, (b) consider their audience and purpose, and focus structure and language accordingly, (c) maintain a consistent voice, (d) proofread carefully. Or whatever goals you want.

The pay-off comes when you get to read a variety of pieces—not thirty half-hearted analytical essays but thirty individual engagements with poetry—and when you get to share a sampling of these different approaches with the class. How do you assess a twelve-line poem in comparison to a three-page essay? You just have to make sure that you—or the class—have designed a rubric that's applicable to both. It can take just as long to craft a poem that measures up to those requirements as to write the prose. In general, I don't grade poems until the student has selected and revised some for a final portfolio; I write comments or hold a conference. But when specific goals are set, there's no reason not to grade a poem, if that's the form the student has committed to.

Problem: A succession of exercises like this takes time. Obviously we can't give every poem such full-dress treatment. But we taught so much here! So much that can be applied to our future reading of poetry and writing about it. So much that will enrich the poems our students go on to create.

Note

1. Robert Bly, *Leaping Poetry* (Boston: Beacon Press, 1975). While Robert Bly's translations are controversial, this book, which contains translations of Cesar Vallejo, Federico García Lorca, and others, along with some contemporary American poets, is also a treatise on how great works of art make rich associations or "leaps" between the conscious and the unconscious. It's very helpful reading, especially for those of us who tend to approach poetry as logical, a riddle with an answer that can be found if we just work hard enough, and who believe that the poet "puts in hidden meanings" on purpose.

Chapter 6

Making Your Poem Concrete

[A]ND FOR THE POET THERE ARE NO IDEAS BUT IN THINGS. . . . THAT IS THE POET'S BUSINESS. NOT TO TALK IN VAGUE CATEGORIES BUT TO WRITE PARTICULARLY, AS A PHYSICIAN WORKS, UPON A PATIENT, UPON THE THING BEFORE HIM, IN THE PARTICULAR TO DISCOVER THE UNIVERSAL.

WILLIAM CARLOS WILLIAMS, *THE AUTOBIOGRAPHY*

You have reacquainted students with their bodies and their physical sensations and have enabled them to experience more sensuously the poems they read on the page. Both these processes should help rescue their own poems from the abyss of abstraction into which teenagers, despite their powerful hormones, are very prone to fall. It's ironic to me that at a time of such aches and ecstasies, students should be so attracted to the abstract. I think they see it as adult territory which they want to enter and possess— like driving a car. To write about "reality," "death," "love," and "truth" gives them a sense of mastery. It's an important stage in their intellectual development. But it can wreak havoc with their poetry.

Some poet once told me that a poem can afford an abstract noun only once every seven lines. Or maybe it was six. Arbitrary as this sounds, it's not bad advice for teenage poets.

A warning: Once you encourage students to write in *concrete* terms about their feelings, you can expect some powerful—and disturbing— poetry. Angry, terrified, lonely, passionate poems about abuse, loss of virginity, alcoholism, rape, pregnancy, suicide, anorexia, homophobia, divorce, AIDS, nervous breakdowns. As we know, even junior high students are experiencing these things—or their friends are. I've come to realize that I must warn my classes that I can respect confidentiality only up to a point. Sometimes a school or state will have already spelled out where that point is. And sometimes the poem is a cry for help.

"Why is the high school literary magazine so full of depressing poems?" one of my colleagues from the elementary school demanded. "Can't they ever write about ball games or caterpillars, like my kids? Why are they always striking poses?" I explain that even when I assign a poem about caterpillars, they can still twist it into a poem about the end of a love affair or a friend's suicide threat, if that's what is on their minds. Georgia Heard, writing poems with elementary children, says to them and their teachers, "Many of my poems begin with a feeling, some deep urge. Sometimes it's so strong I actually feel something inside me move. It can happen any time; it happens about ideas, memories, things I see every day. . . . Poems come from something deeply felt; it's essential for student poets to be able to choose their own topics according to what's important to them." [1]

And this is doubly—triply—true for adolescents. Often, as with adult poets, their topics choose them.

It helps a high school or junior high student to know she need not be alone, she can be part of a community of writers, peers and adults, living and dead, who have not only experienced many of the same joys and sorrows but in writing about them have often found clarity—even comfort. Does this mean that we're treating poetry as therapy rather than as art? (You may not have time to worry about this question, but there is always someone around to spoil your day!) I don't think it's a fruitful question, particularly in working with young writers. Art has always offered a release and clarification of feelings, both to artist and audience. Even the most objective, classically restrained art, by its demands on the creative imagination, absorbs its maker to a degree that can be called therapeutic. One of the typical accusations leveled against adolescents is that they're preoccupied with self to an unhealthy degree. Will writing poems about their emotional experience increase this "self-indulgence," this "egotism"? Not if they're trying to find the best word, the right form, the most memorable images, through which to communicate this experience. Not if we issue a challenge: create poems that a total stranger—say, an adult—will find riveting.

One of my freshmen, who came to us from a very fine school that emphasized poetry, wrote in her final evaluation of our year together:

"Without question, the most important thing I learned in English class this year was to write the truth. Whether or not it was intentional on anyone's part, up until this class I was discouraged by just about anyone who had any say in the matter from writing about the bad, ugly, and hurtful things in my life. I got the overall message that *any* sort of pain I was feeling couldn't be *that* bad. I am not exaggerating in any way when I say that learning to write the truth however bad or ugly it may seem, has completely changed who I am. I have learned that emotions are never 'right' or 'wrong.' . . ."

First, we need to help our students understand that their poems *can* be about serious things, and we can help them find the images and concrete language through which to intuit, think about, and express what's important to them. Then we can move on to helping them widen the range of their concerns, to develop greater empathy and curiosity.

Where to find images? Sometimes an image seizes my attention by evoking an emotion when I least expect it. On the other hand, I may be turning the pages of an art book or a photo album, on a very deliberate quest. Sometimes I start writing about a strong feeling and, out of the physical sensation—or the rhythm and sounds of the first few lines, or a memory that's triggered by the feeling—comes the image I need. Or it may sit up and speak as I'm thumbing through my poetry notebook or going for a run or sitting in a café.

Or working with students. This past winter, about a month after I had lost my mother to cancer, I was giving a workshop to a class of fourth graders, and we were having a good time collecting variants on the word *house*. One girl offered me an image that stayed with me all day and later, that night, started a poem streaming into my notebook:

Somewhere in the Forest of Wild Hands

The children enumerate houses—
igloo, tepee, longhouse, cabin,
skyscraper, shell, cocoon,
"Grave," she says, she is ten
and leads them through the forest of wild hands
to a clearing.
They are thrilled. They are pure vibrato,
how did she think of that?
And I wonder, should we all go back
to "chrysalis," a pretty word,
and what happened to Charlotte when she wove
her sac of spider eggs?
"Grave," she says.
Discovery has so many colors.
Who in here has visited a grave?
I leave it alone, but think how long
a tuning fork will vibrate.
Some day, deep in her own woods
she will think "house," she will think "grave,"
and go with mop and broom, boxes and tears
to her mother's
in search of a clearing.

Would the image of grave as house—common enough, but not on the lips of
a ten-year-old—have reverberated for me in this way if I hadn't been so
wrapped up in my mother's death? I think perhaps images can arrest your
imagination at any time—aesthetically? intellectually?—but to arrest your
heart they have to present themselves at a *particular time.* Stanley Kunitz's
powerful poem "The Portrait," in which he tells of being struck on the cheek
by his mother when he turned up a portrait of his father—who had committed suicide while she was pregnant—was written more than sixty years after
the event. Now in his sixty-fourth year, the poet says, "I can feel my cheek /
still burning." The image, even the physical sensation, of the slap had been
there all his life, growing, waiting, one could say, till his psyche was ready
to explore it in a poem.[2]

Students tend to assume that only the loftiest or most romantic images—stars, flowers, sunsets—can be suitable for poetry, so it helps to show them poems with seemingly mundane images like Williams's red wheelbarrow,[3] Dickinson's loaded gun,[4] Roethke's root cellar,[5] Plath's cut thumb like an onion,[6] and Naomi Shihab Nye's two skunks,[7] given by a man to his wife as a valentine because he thought they were beautiful. My pot holder (chap. 2) just presented itself at the right time and place; but if I hadn't been writing poems for a while, I might not have recognized it as something to write about, as an evocative image for me. I might not have had the confidence to trust my instinct—to sit down then and there and start a poem. I might not have even registered the shiver.

Therefore it's a good idea to thrust potential images at students and give them practice in exploring possible connections between object and emotions. One exercise that I borrowed from two poet/teachers, Toi Derricotte and Madeline Tiger,[8] forces the issue very usefully. Students fold a piece of paper in three vertical columns. *In the first*, they write five emotions they've experienced fairly recently—or any five emotions, one on each line. (With younger classes you may have to clarify what constitutes an emotion, and specify that you want nouns, not adjectives.) They fold this column over, and *in the second* they write five colors—basic primaries or fancier, hyphenated shades like silver-gray. Folding this column over, they then list five animals *in the third column*. Or you can dictate five evocative objects: I often use *knife, star, door, blanket, mirror*—in any order.

Now they unfold the paper, reading across to make five metaphorical statements—five possible opening lines for a poem: For example, *fear is a red door*. That night, they choose one of their lines to explore in an un-rhymed poem, focusing on the emotion and its behavior, its effect on and within them. (Why unrhymed? Because the great rhyme hunt tends to distract students from exploring their images.) Warn everyone to stick with the one emotion they chose, not to incorporate others. If they wish, they can warm up with five minutes of free association on any or all of their three key words—the feeling, the color, and the object.

Try writing your own poem, the same night your students write theirs. It's a good opportunity to indulge in the introspection that we rarely allow ourselves during the teaching day. Force yourself to stick with the metaphor you choose, no matter how unpromising or uncomfortable it begins to feel. Consult your body: what sensations of heaviness, lightness, constriction, release, have you come to associate with this emotion? Respond to the color and object or animal you're working with; what connotations do they have for you? Close your eyes. What pictures come into your mind? Let time feel fluid . . . past, present, future blurring into one another. What memories are emerging? This is your private time. You don't have to share your entire poem with the class; offer a few lines.

Recently, when I did this exercise with a class of freshmen, one girl, new that year and up until now very silent in class, read to us:

> *Gradually*
> *inching closer and closer to you*
> *that indigo blanket*
> *smothers you*
> *leaving you blocked*
> *isolated*
> *from the rest of the world*
> *waiting and waiting*
> *for someone*
> *anyone*
> *to come and notice*
> *this heavy indigo*
> *blanket of loneliness.*

Indigo. Maybe she loved the sound of the word—or maybe her favorite singers were the Indigo Girls. For me the word evokes the loneliness of the blues, and specifically Duke Ellington's "Mood Indigo." Or a dark blue sky, empty of stars. Notice how much the *physical* sensation of loneliness—its heaviness, its smothering quality—contributes to the poem's force. The poet clearly knows what she's talking about. It was no coincidence that loneliness appeared in her list of five emotions. After she had finished reading, other students agreed immediately that yes, this was how it felt to be new— or just to be perceived as different from your peers. That day I remember sensing the class was starting to come together.

And I also learned, during our conference on this poem, that her dad was in prison for abusing her mother, that they had an unlisted phone number, and that her mother was planning to move away as soon as her father was released. No wonder she was feeling "suffocated."

Another freshman girl, tall, quiet, graceful, very self-possessed, startled many of us by writing about lust:

> *Lust is a royal purple knife.*
> *You can see the vivid knife*
> *coming at you with all its glory.*
> *But when it slices*
> *at your soft pink flesh*
> *it is a cruel surprise.*
> *It is stuck in you*
> *and you can't get it out.*

Notice how both these girls can see the emotion approaching and feel powerless to block it, whether it takes them by surprise "in all its glory" or menaces them from afar, "creeping" slowly closer. They recognize the nature of emotion, how inevitably it takes possession. But writing a poem about it enables them to experience the feeling from a perspective that clarifies it and even leads one of them to ask for help: "waiting for someone, anyone, to come and notice."

This exercise nearly always surprises the students, both as poets and audience. For some, it's their first "serious" poem, and they find themselves empowered by the clarity of the initial image to say things they didn't know they knew. They discover how creatively they can "think." And they're impressed with the psychological insights of their peers, sometimes coming to admire classmates whom they'd assumed, for a variety of reasons, were total losers. The level of maturity in the class rises. They start to take one another more seriously as writers and as people.

I also notice some of them begin to associate feeling with color and concrete objects in their subsequent poems. This is a very important development. It's exactly what we want! One boy, small and seemingly young socially for his age (and so totally immersed in sci-fi and fantasy that I thought girls to him were merely Aliens), wrote a poem that took a delightful leap in the last line—and, incidentally, used spacing effectively—to capture the confusion of one's early experience with love. The scene was a picnic and softball game.

I'm mesmerized by her beauty.
Brown hair, eyes soft, fair
We play around
Tease, talk, joke, flirt.
I'm in love   not really   just
deep blue passion.

Working with older students—juniors and seniors—I've found myself engaged in some fascinating discussions when I replace the list of emotions with "men" and "women." You could also replace emotions with themes from whatever work the class happens to be studying; this exercise can pave the way for some very thoughtful essays. Ambition is a . . . Prejudice is a . . .

I've also noticed that writing about an emotion through color and image galvanizes those students who had been convinced that poems have to rhyme to try free verse, where they can say more readily what they feel. As one of my freshmen wrote in the introduction to his portfolio, "I have this slight problem with rhyming. I'm how you say kicking the habit. . . . I used to pinpoint words for rhyme and I believe that I may have forgotten about their reason. . . . I have discovered that it is important to become better acquainted with your feelings."

Once students have opened themselves to the power of free association, imagery, and emotional honesty, I can *then* introduce a range of forms that are fun and challenging to try—the pantoum, the sestina, the villanelle, the sonnet, terza rima, the cinquain. I can encourage them to make up their own forms—by listening to the beginning of a new poem and taking advantage of any promising patterns. But first they must be weaned from forced rhymes that trivialize their efforts and distract them from the experience they want to write about. Particularly if they are to start writing longer poems, in which they probe more deeply the remarkable power of imagery.

Notes

1. Georgia Heard, *For the Good of the Earth and Sun: Teaching Poetry* (Portsmouth, NH: Heinemann, 1989) 10. While this book focuses on the elementary school classroom, it offers much wisdom that can be applied to reading and writing poems with high schoolers. Heard is an experienced poet/teacher

who worked seven years with the Columbia Teachers College Writing Project and now travels throughout the country as a consultant in the teaching of writing. I also highly recommend her second book, especially for those of us who love to write but need encouragement or "jump-start" exercises: *Writing toward Home: Tales and Lessons to Find Your Way* (Heinemann, 1995). If you can secure Georgia Heard for a day-long visit to your school, you will have an experience that resonates with you and your students for a long time.

2. Stanley Kunitz, *Passing Through: The Later Poems, New and Selected* (New York: W. W. Norton, 1995) 22. This collection contains poems from seven decades in the life of one of our most respected poets and mentors of poets. When Kunitz read at the Dodge Poetry Festival, everyone in the big tent rose to their feet. You can hear him read and converse with Bill Moyers on video in *The Power of the Word* (see notes, chap. 1). Students may learn a new respect for old age if they see the different stages and styles of a seventy-year career. His conversation also helps clarify the role of dreams and the unconscious in poetry writing.

3. Williams, "The Red Wheelbarrow," *Collected Poems,* vol. 1, 224 (see note 3, chap. 3).

4. Dickinson, "My Life had stood—a Loaded Gun—" in *The Complete Poems,* #754, 369 (see note 1, chap. 2).

5. Roethke, "Root Cellar" and others from *The Lost Son and Other Poems* in *The Collected Poems,* 35–42 (see note 3, chap. 2).

6. Sylvia Plath, "Cut" in *The Collected Poems* (New York: Harper and Row, Inc.,1960).

7. Naomi Shihab Nye, "Valentine for Ernest Mann" in *Red Suitcase* (Brockport, NY: BOA, 1990).

8. Toi Derricotte and Madeline Tiger, *Creative Writing: A Manual for Teachers* (Trenton, NJ: New Jersey State Council on the Arts). This is a handy little 20-page brochure containing information about bringing poets into the classroom via the state arts council (see how this works in your state), twenty poetry-writing exercises, some answers to "questions teachers often ask," and a brief bibliography. Derricotte and Tiger are both fine published poets with a lot of experience as poets-in-the-schools.

Chapter 7

Expanding the Poem

I WANTED, IF I WAS TO WRITE IN A LARGER WAY THAN OF THE BIRDS AND FLOWERS, TO WRITE ABOUT THE PEOPLE CLOSE ABOUT ME: TO KNOW IN DETAIL, MINUTELY WHAT I WAS TALKING ABOUT—TO THE WHITES OF THEIR EYES, TO THEIR VERY SMELLS.

WILLIAM CARLOS WILLIAMS, *THE AUTOBIOGRAPHY*

At this point it's important to build on your class's initial excitement with imagery. The color/animal poems tend to be short; many students aren't sure how a poem moves. It's not the same as a story, is it? Here, just as the Shakespeare recitations gave you a chance to look at dramatic monologues, the students' confusion offers opportunities to look at narrative poetry. To understand anything, examine what it *isn't*. Junior high students, especially, like ballads and "story poems"—Robert Service's "Cremation of Sam McGee,"[1] Ernest Thayer's "Casey at the Bat."[2] These can be presented orally by you and the class; they require little discussion time, and can lead to lively writing.

Older, more sophisticated students can, if properly conditioned, enjoy Coleridge's "Rime of the Ancient Mariner."[3] I spend a week and a half on this poem in my semester-long poetry course, including one period for hearing Richard Burton's flamboyant reading of it and some time for presentation of student projects—paintings, choreography, sound collages, dramatic readings. (There was the time the candles and the burning paper heart nearly set the room on fire and did set off the corridor smoke detector—but I don't wish to discourage you!) You can try excerpts from Byron's brilliant satire *Don Juan*,[4] Frost's mix of narrative, dialogue, and lyric in "Home Burial,"[5] and even, for energetic readers, Vikram Seth's verse novel, *The Golden Gate*,[6] about the lives and loves of young professionals in 1980s San Francisco.

It's important to help students make the distinction between narrative and lyric if they're to begin writing longer poems about whatever's on their mind and in their hearts. Emphasize that the lyric focuses on the emotional and sensuous content of an experience, not on the sequence of events, though developing the experience in detail may feel rather like storytelling.

The lyric is the poetic genre most congenial to poets writing in English today—actually, from the nineteenth century on, though there are many more kinds of music and voices now than in the past century. While the lyric is traditionally short, it contains room for rich detail, a complex braiding of time—past, present, and future, for conversation between different voices or selves, and for wild, exhilarating, sometimes bewildering leaps of free association.

I remember the first poem I wrote in which I could feel myself progressing by "leaps." I had invited my freshmen on their final exam to explore their personal connections to the term's reading—Greek mythology and *Romeo and Juliet*. Making my way through piles of essays on a sweaty June morning, I came to Kay's: "A love story is always a descent . . . Juliet dares to die in the dark. She loves so hard she stabs herself right through the heart. I'd do it too." Next came a paragraph about how being in love had helped her grow up: "Definitely I've matured. I know what matters now." She was a very bright, popular girl, so pretty and lively that she attracted the older boys and was repeatedly getting grounded by her parents for the weekend. She went around with a senior whom she hoped to redeem from bad habits, including drunken driving . I kept dreading to hear that she'd been killed in a car crash. As I read her essay, I started to cry, and suddenly a poem emerged with a passion and ease I'd never before experienced when writing. Images seemed to leap out of the pencil, and I had no sense of time passing.

As I was writing the poem, I realized that Kay's words and my worries about her had coalesced with a run I'd taken a day ago and a smell that I'd assumed was that of a dead deer—not unusual in our woods. The invisible deer associated itself with Kay's very visible feelings and with the blood I imagined on the leaves where the deer must lie hidden, and the crows that would eventually find the body. Another leap—to the bird that had flown into my windshield a week ago. And back to my worries about the drunken driving and Kay's vulnerability. The leap from an embroidered heart to a raw, bleeding one startled me, but I didn't pause for thought, just wrote it down.

Final Exams

> Fourteen, and unlike the deer screened by June leaves
> whose death I smell as I pass a certain stretch of woods,
> she wears her red heart boldly
> on her tee-shirt front, more or less where it ought to be.
> Not silkscreened or appliquéd
> or embroidered, but genuinely, adolescently
> raw, the great aorta bleeding fresh from where
> she snapped it off with small, impatient hands.
> "A love story is always a descent,"
> she writes. The words burst out of the bluebook. "Juliet
> dares to die in the dark. She loves so hard
> she stabs herself right through the heart. I'd
> do it too." (Deer's blood mats the leaves.
> Not till the giant crows hover
> will I know where that quick heart died.)
> She searched the ranks of the older boys. "Definitely
> I've matured. I know what matters now." Ask
> whoever is blond and blind and drives the bluest streak.

Explaining how a poem takes shape always feels artificial, I think, to the reader—and to the writer as well. It takes away from the mystery. And there are aspects of the process that defy explanation. But students need to realize, preferably through their own experience but also through hearing other poets talk about their writing processes, that the growth of a poem differs radically from, say, the structuring of a lab report.

The easiest challenge for students who want to start writing longer poems is developing a situation in greater detail. Compare these two poems, both by junior girls, one who's writing about a breakup with her boyfriend and one who's remembering the first time she danced with her father. Both poems are full of genuine emotion and are rooted in physical sensation.

> *I am between screaming and crying*
> *and I want to know*
> *where has all the laughter gone?*
> *I fear I'll never touch the sunshine of your hair or*
> *be taken in by the warmth of your eyes.*
> *I am tormented by memories of yesterdays and*
> *dreams of tomorrows*
> *and I ask, do you still love me? do you ever think of me?*
> *I feel I've spent a lifetime in your arms.*
> *If you could just touch me once more, tell me you'll*
> *never forget me, that's all I need*

The sensations of screaming and crying, of touching the boy's bright, warm hair, of feeling warmed by the expression in his eyes, and yearning for the comfort (physical and emotional) of his embrace, all register on us. The tension of painful remembering and yearning (felt in the repeated questions) is also very physical. But the vagueness, the lack of those details that could individualize this relationship for us, and the clichéd "memories of yesterdays and dreams of tomorrows" in place of concrete imagery make this more like a diary entry, a private catharsis. Interestingly, the author didn't choose this as a poem to revise for her portfolio—I think it had served its purpose, and she liked it the way it was.

One of the advantages in offering formal criticism and grades only to poems the student chooses to revise and make public in her portfolio is that in reading her other pieces we—the feared, clinical "experts"—can pay more attention to *strengths*. This means that in the early stages, we can teach primarily by reinforcement, making a few gentle suggestions about weak line breaks, excessive, imprecise adjectives or dull verbs, the unnecessary clutter of prepositional phrases—but praising the arresting first line, the specific details, the unexpected and absolutely on-target metaphor. We don't have to assign a grade. This approach encourages students to risk writing about what they really feel and sharing it with us. I hate to catch myself sounding like Polonius in criticizing a sixteen-year-old's love poem—"'To the celestial, and my soul's idol, the most beautified Ophelia,'—/ That's an ill phrase, a vile phrase, 'beautified' is a vile phrase."

Here's the second girl's poem, "First Dance":

> *He spun me*
> *in circles, I was drunk with dizziness.*
> *I looked up at my father.*
> *He smiled,*
> *I blushed, turned away.*
> *He guided me in the box-step*
> *gently*
> *so my small legs could keep up.*
> *I smelled the ocean,*
> *dinner, smooth moist air.*
> *I smelled my father's after-shave,*
> *steel drum music*
> *vibrating like bells in my ears.*
> *He held my right hand*
> *with a steady grip.*
> *My arm hugged his middle.*
> *It did not matter what the others thought.*
> *We danced*
> *Forever.*

Here the author has not only grounded her feelings firmly in a kines-thetic memory—the dizziness from being spun around, the efforts of a child to keep step with a much bigger adult, and the gentle, guiding touch of her father's hands—oh, and don't forget that fine, telling blush when he smiles at her; she has also grounded us in the smells and sounds of a specific moment, which help "put us there," individualize the relationship between father and daughter, and make us believe in its emotional significance to the

speaker. She has taken pains to invite us into the world of her poem, and we
return the compliment by investing our senses and empathy: we imagine
the father's feelings, the little girl's thrilled pride and sense of romance, how
amusing or "cute" the couple may have looked to those "others" as they
watched indulgently—and what it means to a sixteen-year-old girl to "dance
Forever" with her father. Later, in conference, I learned that her parents had
divorced when she was little and she now lived with her mother and stepfa-
ther. Writing this poem helped her resurrect and intensify a memory she very
much wanted to keep. It may also have helped her understand it more fully.

When a poem describes a personal experience in more or less colloquial
free verse, the question may arise, "Isn't this just like a prose description?
Does it gain from being written out in lines like this?" Try putting the previous poem into a paragraph:

> He spun me in circles, I was drunk with dizziness. I looked up at
> my father. He smiled, I blushed, turned away. He guided me in the
> box step gently so my small legs could keep up. I smelled the
> ocean, dinner, smooth moist air. I smelled my father's after-shave,
> steel drum music vibrating like bells in my ears. He held my right
> hand with a steady grip. My arm hugged his middle. It did not
> matter what the others thought. We danced forever.

How much of the evocative power is lost by not slowing us down to linger
over certain isolated details—"I looked up at my father / He smiled, / I
blushed." This is an important exchange, which the poem's lineation makes
us look at and think about as if it were a photograph in a frame. Look at the
long, run-on line that follows the opening—"He spun me / in circles, I was
drunk with dizziness." In the preceding, short, monosyllabic line we already
see a circle; the unexpected break (enjambment) disorients us a little, and
in the second, panting, spinning, run-on line the circles multiply so we join
the child in her "drunken" dizziness. Breaking up the description of their
partnering into three lines—"He held my right hand / with a steady grip /
My arm hugged his middle"—helps make us slow down and register this in
our own bodies remembering what it feels like to be steadied by an older,
bigger person whom you literally and figuratively look up to. And putting
the final word of the poem, "forever," on a line by itself signals very clearly
what it meant—and means—to the daughter, as she looks back on this

memory. The sound of the word is left to vibrate in the surrounding blank space, as in Keats's "Ode to a Nightingale" where a similar sound, the word "forlorn," is placed at the end of one line and repeated at the start of the next, to echo in the air—"to toll me back to my sole self."

"First Dance" was written in a junior elective I sometimes teach called Men and Women in Literature. Since I incorporate poetry reading and poetry writing into all my courses, I suggested, after we'd read a packet of poems dealing with relationships between the sexes, that we each think about the different types of relationships we'd had with the opposite sex—sons with mothers, sisters with brothers, romantic relationships, friendships, etc.—and pick one to explore in a poem. I stressed the importance of grounding these poems in a specific moment and recreating the moment, in all its emotion, through sensuous details of place and time and physical sensations. I also urged attention to the visual and aural effect of line breaks.

One senior boy responded with a piece very definitely grounded in the physical. His poem made it into the school literary magazine only over strenuous opposition from the administration! My freshmen, sprawled on the classroom floor to devour the new issue of the magazine, were impressed by the poem. They talked about how much more "serious" it made sex seem. It felt "real." I think that despite its powerful sensuality and violent emotions, "First Time" offered a safer model for these younger students than all the casual, often violent, sex they saw in the movies and on MTV, because it does take the relationship seriously.

First Time

> You spread your legs in
> a dark promise
> to let me in
> I saw your life,
> like a moist photograph,
> your memories engraved in sacred flesh.
> Inside
> the machinery clanked and whirred
> unborn children wanted out of their prison
> and my need rushed in

pumping
staining your emptiness.
Beneath those mouthless, darkened lips
lies my innocence
shed like an ancient skin.

Afterwards

you whispered that I'd grow to hate you
but after I felt your life pulse around me
like a glove
the scream of our melting flesh bonded us.
We can never be strangers again.

This poem was not read aloud in class. But, clearly, the author felt committed to it, committed enough to revise it with me and submit it to the magazine. How do we, as teachers, respond to such a poem? If we praise it, are we also saying that we wholeheartedly endorse sexual relationships between sixteen-year-olds? Whether we discuss the issue with the student depends on our own feelings and the kind of relationship we have with him. But I think we have to respond to the courage, the respect for self and partner, and the love of writing that led the student to transform this important experience into poetry. The images of the moist photograph and the girl's life pulsing around his like a glove, the careful choice of adjectives and verbs, the arrangement in stanzas, and the movement from the girl's initial "dark promise" to the writer's sense of having sealed a bond—all reflect an intense respect for human feeling and for language, for art. If we can teach or reinforce these two things through poetry, surely it's worth the risk of letting the body enter the classroom.

Notes

1. Robert Service, *The Spell of the Yukon* (New York: Putnam Publishing Group, 1989).

2. Ernest Thayer's "Casey at the Bat" may be found in *The Best Loved Poems of the American People*, compiled by Hazel Felleman (New York: Doubleday and Co., Inc., 1936).

3. Samuel Taylor Coleridge, *The Rime of the Ancient Mariner and Other Poems* (New York: Dover, 1992). I recommend this paperback Dover Thrift Edition, because "The Ancient Mariner" is generally not anthologized due to length and takes forever to photocopy. To introduce the poem I have the class listen with me to part of the taped reading by Richard Burton, John Neville, and Robert Hardy from Musical Heritage Society, 1710 Highway 35, Ocean, NJ 07712 (MHC 6716L). The tape also includes "Kubla Khan" and "Christabel." For visuals, Gustave Dore's forty-two illustrations of the poem are very exciting (New York: Dover, 1970).

4. George Gordon, Lord Byron, *Don Juan* (Cambridge, MA: Riverside Press, 1958).

5. Robert Frost, "Home Burial" in *Complete Poems* (New York: Holt, Rinehart and Winston, 1964) 69–73.

6. Vikram Seth, *Golden Gate* (New York: Random House, 1991).

Chapter 8

Hand-Eye Coordination

HARVEST MOON—

WALKING AROUND THE POND

ALL NIGHT LONG.

MATSUO BASHŌ, TRANSLATED BY ROBERT HASS

A respect for language . . . But sometimes the hand is quicker than the eye. It grabs the pencil and slaps down an adjective before the eye has finished looking. The day is "lovely": full of "fluttering" leaves and "sparkling" waves; clouds sail by, "cotton-white" and, in short, as Alexander Pope said some two-and-a-half centuries ago in his "Essay on Criticism":

> "Where'er you find 'the cooling western breeze,'
> In the next line, it 'whispers through the trees;'
> If crystal streams 'with pleasing murmurs creep,'
> The reader's threatened (not in vain) with 'sleep';"

We've asked our students to write poems that invite us to enter. To ground us in concrete, physical detail. To stop, look, and listen. But in the excitement of the moment—in the flush of inspiration—*my* leaves are prone to flutter; and "dark" is my all-time favorite adjective. The four other senses get robbed of their rights, too, but we rely more for imagery on *sight* than on any of the others, so it suffers the most. And it doesn't help if you keep losing your bifocals.

How can we dramatize for student poets the importance of taking a closer look?

At the end of a course, I ask students to write a journal entry about a class or assignment that they found memorable. Recently, Katherine, a junior in the poetry elective, wrote:

> This course has forced me to look at things in a very different way than I have seen them before. One class that stands out in my mind is the one when we read Buson's haiku 'On a one-ton temple bell / a luna moth folded in sleep.' You had us close our eyes, relax our bodies and clear our heads. Then you asked us to picture in detail this image: the textures, temperatures, sizes, colors, sounds, smells. Afterward we shared our own images of Buson's poem. Then we each got a marble from the box you brought in and wrote down phrases that came to mind as we looked at our marble. I remember feeling like time had stopped during that class. For forty minutes I forgot about everything else in my life, all the stress and anticipation left me. Focusing so clearly on something so insignificant and small pushed me to call on all of my senses. I learned that this is the primary step to writing strong poetry and creating vivid images.
>
> Then you took us into New York. I have been to the city many times, but walking around Manhattan with our poetry class I felt like I was seeing the city for the first time. You gave us little notebooks and told us this was our camera and to take many photographs. For the first time I really opened my eyes and noticed specific people on the street. I observed how they walked, who they walked with, how they dressed. I noticed one woman slumped over in the passenger seat with her feet resting on the dashboard, her window half rolled down, waiting for someone to return to the car. On any other day I would have passed right by her and she would have faded into the blur of all the passing people. That day I noticed the color of the hot dog signs on the vendors' wagons. I

noticed a fern growing on the shaded window sill of a third floor apartment. I paid attention to my other senses too: the stench of urine that reeked in the subway tunnels; the screaming police sirens I heard from Central Park Zoo. My notebook by the end of the afternoon was a collage of images of ordinary life in New York City. But the experience for me was out of the ordinary.

This is the student who wrote the poem about dancing with her boy cousins, "Half Dance Afternoon," quoted at the beginning of chapter 3. I wish I had asked her how she got from the class on Buson and the marbles to learning "that this is the primary step to writing strong poetry and creating vivid images"! Like Katherine, I find this kind of attentiveness "out of the ordinary" and would like it to become more a part of my daily life. I want it for my students, too, especially because I agree with artist Frederick Franck that it's closely connected to empathy: "When the eye wakes up to see again, it suddenly stops taking anything for granted. The thing I draw, be it leaf, rosebush, woman or child, is no longer a thing, no longer my 'object' over and against which I am the supercilious 'subject.' The split is healed. When I am drawing leaf or caterpillar or human face, it is at once de-thingified. I say yes to its existence. By drawing it, I dignify it, I declare it worthy of total attention, as worthy of attention as I am myself, for sheer existence is the awesome mystery and miracle we share."[1]

Before experimenting with the haiku exercise, which can be a stretch for the more literal-minded student ("Big deal—I see this moth on this bell"), you may want to have your class bring in objects to study—to draw and write about. I usually insist on something organic that they can envision in successive stages of its life. I ask them to set the object on their desk and close their eyes for a minute. "When your eyes open, imagine you are seeing this object for the first time. In fact, imagine this is the first such object to appear on the earth and you are the first one to see it. Naturally, you'll look at it very closely, poke it a bit, shake it, sniff it . . .

Now you want to make a record of it. Here is a piece of paper. Take your pencil and, *without looking at your paper*—not even once, not even a sidelong glance—draw the object in detail. Don't stop looking at it. The point is not to make a perfect drawing but to get to know your object as fully as possible—every vein and dimple, every speck and abrasion, every shadow and crevice. Think large, as you start to draw, because you'll be putting in so many details and you won't be able to see exactly where on the paper you're putting them. This is a case where process, not product, is the significant thing."

Expect a lot of groaning. Eighth and ninth graders tend to be more obsessed with making a "realistic," accurate drawing than juniors and seniors, who may have been exposed in art class or museum trips to abstract art and the power of distortion to express truth. If you're drawing your own object—which is a good thing to do—check, especially at the outset, to be sure people aren't sneaking a look at their paper. The temptation is overwhelming! You can be a good role model; hold up your own art work, laugh at it, but point out the things you discovered about your object that you hadn't noticed before. As I write this, I've been taking a lot of time out to watch the red squirrel on my window ledge. I just caught him in the act of yawning. At least, he stretched and opened his mouth very wide; it sure looked like a yawn.

We tend to see what we want to see. What we're used to seeing. Last week as I said goodbye to my Men and Women in Lit. group, I asked how many, in the course of the semester we'd spent together, had changed their assumptions about at least one person in the class. Every hand, including mine, went up. But challenging our assumptions had been one of the avowed purposes of that course; it had been a frequent subject for discussion. Whether it's the opposite sex or squirrels or dry leaves, we instinctively classify and judge as quickly as possible, in order to move on to the next item demanding our attention. Poets and artists can't afford to do this.

Moving from visual to verbal, I ask the class to start listing words—right on their drawings—that capture as precisely as possible what their senses have been telling them and what they have tried to draw. Sometimes we first make five lists on the board of "sense" words, just to warm up:

> *touch*—gritty damp silken furry hairy sticky squishy pulpy dusty
> *sound*—rustle peep bubble whisper crackle
> *sight*—oblong curly spiked undulating minuscule oval notched
>   indented veined striated
> *smell*—spicy earthy sour sweet piney musty astringent piercing
> *taste*—bland hot crunchy grainy syrupy mealy sweet spicy

We note how the senses blur so that one word will often apply to more than one sense. We mention *onomatopoeia*—crunch, crack, grunt. We puzzle how to describe the taste of a stone, the sound of a piece of bark or of a mushroom. I might read them Sylvia Plath's poem about mushrooms—the soft "insistent" hands "taking hold of the loam," whispering their way up through the earth. We agree that finding the right word is very hard work. So is finding a fresh comparison. "Imagine you're the only person on earth to have seen this object; you want to leave an accurate record for posterity."[2]

Once we've filled our drawings with words, I take the class through a series of questions, expanding from this matter-of-fact study of the object into association, memory, fantasy—different kinds of "seeing," which, along with their initial observations, should help them write a poem for the next class.

> Tell your object some of the things you noticed about it.
>
> List associations you have with your object and its name.
>
> Jot down a memory that your object calls up.
>
> List things you could do with your object.
>
> List some places you would not expect to find your object.
>
> Imagine what it might do in such a place. (Be surprising, outrageous.)
>
> Ask it a few questions or let it ask you some questions.
>
> Offer some answers or answer with another question.
>
> Describe its transformation into something else or some other form of itself.

As they get up to leave, I tell them they don't have to incorporate all this material into their poem; they can select and develop just a couple of items if they'd rather. Given the range of these directives, their poem has the potential to be a humorous fantasy, a memory poem, a dream poem, a nature poem—but however it turns out, it will be grounded in close observation and some precise language. As a sample, here's the beginning of my own, as yet uncompleted, poem based on observing and drawing a pair of otters at the Central Park Zoo. I made detailed notes on shape, size, color, and texture, but in the end it was their *motions* that really stirred my imagination.

One rests his chin on the other's wet flank,
lovers afloat and fluid with late afternoon,
lovers in their slipping streamy protean
flexes, backslidings, Moebius strips.
Eelslick, sealflip, webfoot, rattail, whiskered
as cats, their love is checkered light, silver dark.
They know each other almost as they know
water. I'd like to ask, "How did you learn
this acqueouscence?"

Next day we are ready to share our drafts. But before students read their
poems aloud to the class, I ask everyone to listen particularly for words and
phrases that reveal a fully awakened, an unusually attentive eye so that
when the poem's over I can list these on the board for us to think about.
Then, to set the tone, I read aloud from John Moffitt's poem "To Look at
Any Thing."[3]

To look at any thing,
If you would know that thing,
You must look at it long:
To look at this green and say
'I have seen spring in these
Woods,' will not do . . . .

"Don't assume you've really seen any of the objects you're hearing about
in these poems. Be prepared to see them differently. Assume that you've
never seen the green of a spring wood before."

As we listen to the poems, a record of the students' "seeing" goes up on
the board: *a saltine's eyelet lace, dying banana like a limp, black crescent moon,
the white web spun tight around the orange's flesh, a leaf's busy perforations, a
freckled stone, the saltine orderly as a bingo card, the candle's syrupy drip, a
prune wrinkled as old gums.*

This is the point in their writing when some students suddenly start
keeping a poetry notebook. So if the weather's good, take the class on a walk
to collect textures, smells, sounds, shapes, colors, and interesting juxtaposi-
tions of objects. Who knows which of these may trigger a poem? Or a good
line? But even if none do, it's useful practice in seeing. Students can collect

actual objects or capture them in quick sketches and words. You can also assign them to do this at home; basement and attic (though these poetic conveniences are fast disappearing from the scene), kitchen and backyard and garage are all possible sources. So is the local supermarket, especially the fresh produce section, and, if you live in a city, outdoor flower or vegetable stands. One of my colleagues did a class walk with guests from the first grade; his seniors were startled at how much more interesting familiar terrain becomes when you're seeing it through the eyes of a child. How many more times you have to stop!

Any situation that changes the way you normally perceive your surroundings is apt to be good for your poetry. Falling in love, falling out of love, having a child, starting a new job, travel, acquiring a new skill. Think how many writers got their start when confined to bed during a long childhood illness. A few summers ago I attended a writing workshop in the Pacific Northwest just ten days after I'd had surgery. We were given a daily assignment in "available seeing." In our notebooks we were to record ordinary sights—a slant of light on a diving bird's tail, a hair curled in the still-wet shower drain. Not impose our personality on the thing with fancy figurative language or sound effects but just be attentive, in the spirit of Zen, to its "as-is-ness." Happily, my usual impatience was checked by the fact that I could walk only very slowly, for very short distances. I found myself quite content to sit down on the nearest driftwood log and watch one patch of shore for half an hour. I even became a better reader of haiku.

I show a page from that summer's journal to my senior writers:

> sandal straps limp and lopsided from damp sea air
> sour smell of kelp mixed with wild sweet pea
> small boy in red clings halfway up the bluff over the beach
> hidden dips in smooth sand
> sea gull footprints make umbrella shapes in wet sand

I tell them that while I was pleased to find myself paying more attention to my surroundings, I wasn't convinced at the time that these were useful observations. They seemed so random and their language so matter-of-fact. But a month later, as I read over the page, I began to write a poem about recovering from surgery. To my surprise, four of the five journal entries made their way into the poem:

Each morning I walk a little farther,
listening to my new body ripen
and ache. It makes a green music.
I walk carefully, as if packed full of seeds,
but I am hollow and untried,
like a newly strung guitar.
The ground is my rhythm—
anthill, pebble, pothole, and root
direct my going. Hidden dips in a smooth lawn
assault my body's tenderness like a stranger's hand on my arm.

I cry at the deep impress of a seagull's feet
in wet sand, because it looks like a small umbrella.
I cry when someone says Washington State
has the fourth highest incarceration rate in the nation,
because I love its coffee and its veils of rain.

I am a cracked egg in boiling water.
My first day here I saw from the car a wild beach,
dark under high bluffs, and I wept
at what I couldn't smell from the window—
sun on thistle and sweetpea and sour kelp.
Finally today I walked there: the tide was in,
and some ravens, and one small boy in red halfway up the bluff.
I cried—there was such a narrow strip to walk on,
or maybe because I'd gotten the smells right.

One student said, "It seems like your seeing really made the poem happen." I think that's because once you start paying attention to what you considered small, insignificant things, you become more attentive to everything and come to realize that *nothing* is insignificant—except to the egotist. This is the viewpoint necessary for writing haiku, and it was Basho who said to distrust all adjectives of degree.

Writing haiku is a wonderful discipline for any writer—not only a poet but anyone who wants to cultivate attentiveness to the world and to language. But it's very difficult to do well. I once spent a four-hour plane flight trying to rub two images together to produce a "spark" in three lines. And a whole morning that had been designed for housecleaning got devoted to reducing the cluttered apartment to my vision of Japanese simplicity in these lines:

I dream emptiness:
bare floor,
   sun in a bowl.

If you do want to take the time to write haiku with your class, browse through William Higginson's wonderfully thorough *Haiku Handbook,*[4] and immerse yourself in a good anthology, such as Robert Hass's recent translations, *The Essential Haiku.* But rather than write haiku with the whole class, you might choose simply to read some aloud together and then give special help to anyone who really wants to try his hand at it.

The exercise Katherine described is one I've done with ten-year-olds as well as seniors. Seated quietly in a circle on the floor with their eyes closed, having just focused for a few minutes on their breathing, students listen to me read Buson's lines that invite us to see a luna moth sleeping with folded wings on a one-ton temple bell. I read it several times, or ask someone else to read it after me. We sit silently for a minute. Then, keeping our eyes closed, we go around the circle saying what our senses and associations gave us as we listened to the poem. Responses range from memories of a trip to Japan or to a museum, to readings for a religion course, to an image of the startled moth flying away as the bell is rung, to an appreciation of the textural contrast between the fragile wings and the heavy bronze or iron, to the juxtaposition of an ancient bell with an ephemeral insect, to a suggestion that both objects are sleeping . . . .

The students realize, if they hadn't before now, that everyone heard a different poem, based in part on her own experiences and her predilections for one sense over the other, for space over time, for philosophy over art. "Suppose I had used a different translation," I ask, "with no reference to the folded wings or the weight of the bell? What would your imagination have supplied, do you think?"

Appreciating haiku calls for the same attentiveness as drawing an object and then finding the precise words to describe what we've seen. It's just that process in reverse. If we can pay attention to three lines of poetry—really see what the poet has "drawn"—we should be able to read longer poems with the same empathic attentiveness.

At this point it can be helpful to ask students to make a painting or collage of the images in a somewhat longer poem. Collage is particularly rich in possibilities if you insist that students choose a variety of textures and shapes and layerings to capture not only literal textures and shapes that may be mentioned or implicit in the images (and the shape of the poem on the page?) but also the "feel" of the poem—the poet's tone. This requires careful, imaginative reading, silently and aloud. It's also a good idea to get the class brainstorming a list of materials and objects with interesting, evocative texture that they might use—sand paper, cotton, silver foil, plastic wrap, brown paper bags, rubber bands, nails, string, ribbon, strands of hair, lipstick, etc. Given the declining number of art programs in the schools, it may be wise to get a list of shapes up on the board, too, and show examples of collage—to lift it out of the realm of glued cut-outs from teen fashion and sports magazines.

I've used Wallace Stevens's "Disillusionment at Ten O'Clock," Gary Snyder's "Four Poems for Robin," e. e. cummings's "in Just-," Coleridge's "Rime of the Ancient Mariner"—there are lots of possibilities.[5] You can hang the collages on the wall and combine art show with poetry reading. If you make it clear that this work is to be taken seriously, you can get students to "read" one another's collages, once they've heard the relevant poems: "I like the way you made the rhododendron blossoms bigger than lifesize and kind of transparent with the plastic wrap, because in the poem they're real flowers but they're falling while the guy's asleep so maybe he's dreaming them, too—and they could be, like, a symbol of this old girlfriend he misses. And you made the beach out of sandpaper, which is a good contrast to the plastic wrap, like it's nitty gritty reality." "Yes, and the beach goes off to the back of the paper like it goes on forever—it's the rest of his life without her" (Gary Snyder's "Four Poems for Robin").

Or they can write journal entries or even essays about the connections they see between poem and collage. The main point is, once again, to slow them down and intensify their experience of encountering a poem.

Notes

1. Frederick Franck, *Zen Seeing, Zen Drawing: Meditation in Action* (New York: Bantam/Doubleday, 1993) xvii. An important book for every poet and poetry lover to own. To quote from the jacket: "Franck encourages us to pick up a

pencil so that after years of merely looking at the world around us, we see it again as if for the first time. Filled with wise and moving autobiographical recollections, Zen stories, quotations, koans, proverbs, anecdotes about his students' breakthroughs, and Franck's own beautiful pen-and-ink views of the world," this book "will renew and refresh those who draw as well as those who do not."

2. Sylvia Plath, "Mushrooms" in *The Collected Poems* (New York: Harper & Row, 1981) 139.

3. John Moffitt in *Reflections on a Gift of Watermelon Pickle . . . and Other Modern Verse*, ed. Dunning, Lueders, and Smith (Glenville, IL: Scott, Foresman and Co., 1966) 21. Many of us who came of age as teachers in the sixties still love and use this anthology, which is, unfortunately, out of print. Moffitt's poem may be found in other collections.

4. William J. Higginson with Penny Harter, *The Haiku Handbook: How to Write, Share, and Teach Haiku* (New York: Kodansha America, Inc., 1985). An invaluable paperback reference and anthology that includes material on the form (along with the tanka), a brief history of haiku traditional and modern, and samples by Japanese, American, and European poets ranging from the four best-known masters—Bashō, Buson, Issa, and Shiki—to skilled contemporary American haiku writers like Geraldine Clinton Little. There are several helpful chapters on how to read and write haiku with students, and an interesting list of traditional "season words" or kigo—plants, animals, weather, rituals—arranged by season. Students who have suffered in elementary school from syllable counting and workbook formulae ("fill in a spring flower, a color, an emotion") can be converted by exposure to some of the modern American examples and by Higginson's down-to-earth attitude: "Haiku happens all the time, wherever there are people who are 'in touch' with the world of their senses, and with their own feeling response to it."

Keeping a sketchbook/notebook during different times of year can help sensitize some students to the clarity of haiku, and for those who are convinced their haiku have to be about pretty, peaceful scenes, read them Michael McClintock's poem, anthologized in *The Haiku Handbook* (see above):

> *dead cat . . .*
> *open mouthed*
> *to the pouring rain*

My own two favorite books for capturing the essence of haiku are *A Zen Wave* by Robert Aitken (New York: Weatherhill, Inc., 1978) and Sam Hamill's *Basho's Ghost* (Seattle: Broken Moon Press, 1989). Each little chapter of *A Zen Wave* is an intimate, thoughtful talk by Aitken, one of the first American Zen masters, who studied Japanese poetry and Zen in Japan, and each talk focuses on one of Basho's haiku—its spirit, its language, some of the different translations.

Gary Snyder writes that Aitken "illuminates the angles and corners of loneness and community, plainness and beauty, in the homey, homeless way of Zen." Hamill, a poet, translator, student of Japanese culture, and the founder of Copper Canyon Press, travels through parts of northern Japan where Basho made his journeys three hundred years ago, seeking the poet's spirit in poets and artists he meets along the way, in the places and objects of which Basho wrote, and in his own responses to the world he encounters. A very moving book.

This is also the place to recommend poet Robert Hass's translations of Bashō, Buson, and Issa—*The Essential Haiku* (Hopewell, NJ: The Ecco Press, 1994), which contains about a hundred poems by each writer and an introductory sketch of each. Hass writes that he has tried to give us "the variety and intensity of experience this small form can sustain. What is in these poems can't be had elsewhere. About the things of the world, and the mind looking at the things of the world, and the moments and the language in which we try to express them, they have unusual wakefulness and clarity."

5. Short lyrics by Stevens, Snyder, and cummings, along with excellent, flexible writing suggestions, may all be found very conveniently in Kenneth Koch's and Kate Farrell's fine anthology and poetry teaching manual, *Sleeping on the Wing* (see note 9, chap. 3). This is a classic that should be on every high school poetry teacher's bookshelf.

Words Words Words

J just can't put it into words." In moments of strong feeling, or profound revelation, even poets get impatient with the limitations of words. Shelley, striving to render the essence of a cloud or a skylark and the ineffable feelings they stirred in him, practically expired with frustration. But words, with their rich freight of connotation and sound, the feelings they can stir merely from the physical sensation of saying them, let alone the personal associations they acquire for us through music, reading, living, are a remarkable medium.

Like sensory awareness, comfort with our bodies, and active, imaginative reading, the joy of acquiring language seems to fade as we get more educated. When I visit a kindergarten class, the "word of the day" is up on the easel, and the children are improvising sentences with it. Their teacher goes on to tell them about the maypole dance, and I overhear one boy mouthing to himself, "maypole . . . maple . . . maple leaf . . . maple sugar." When we first learn the names for things, we go around triumphantly naming and pointing, believing perhaps that when we say "sun" the sun appears. As we learn to read, the *sensation* of connecting the shapes of the letters B E A R with the sounds our mouth is making and the picture on the page and the actual object we've seen—our teddy bear, or the bear at the zoo—and our memory of someone older reading that very page to us and, maybe, our anticipation of that word even before the right page is turned, all add up to something—well, sensational!

For many of us, the physical act of writing the letters ourselves, and the fear of misspelling, which surfaces all too soon in many classrooms, along with the sense that it's much easier to say the words than write them, erode our initial excitement over words. But in my experience, up through fifth grade it's still relatively easy to rekindle this enthusiasm. By junior high, many other factors conspire against it, among which are standard vocabulary workbooks and tests and later, of course, the dreaded Verbal sections on the College Boards and the cramming they inspire—as opposed to the more natural, easy acquisition and analysis of words in the context of, say, writing poetry.

I've known teachers to identify a word as worthy of attention by referring to it as "a College Board word." These words tend to be Latin derivatives with very little appeal to the senses and emotions. While high school is the time when one is concentrating on classifying and reasoning, so the mastery of the mostly Latinate words which we use in these processes is useful, a poem made up primarily of such words as *implicit, inference, cogitate, cerebrate, eclectic,* and *erudite* would probably not stir the pulses.

To fall in love with reading and writing poems, we have to fall in love with the richness of language—not just our little cache of words that we use daily or encounter in *Time* magazine, but words from every period of history, from the worlds of music, cooking, biology, astronomy, geography, computers, journalism, advertising, religions, words from foreign languages and the slang and dialects of other parts of the country. Poets know this, though each draws from his own particular hoard. With Quincy Troupe you get what he calls "the living language" of the streets and bars and prisons and slaughterhouses, of jazz and basketball, all in the Black idiom[1]; with

Pattiann Rogers the names of plants and animals and biological processes[2]; with Alice Fulton, physics and mathematics[3]; with A. R. Ammons, geology and natural history.[4] With Shakespeare, words from law, medicine, the theater, astrology, government, music—and a wealth of new forms he coined in the fire of his impatient imagination. With Gerard Manley Hopkins, more invention, a wild stream of hyphenated celebration—like "fresh-firecoal chestnut-falls." Whitman pours out a democratic potpourri that makes you want to grab your pencil and write a poem on the spot: *gibberish, muck, mast-hemmed, bull's eye, accoucheur, manure, oscillate, biscuits, contralto, egress, piazza, tote, Chattahoochee, promulges, Ahoy, sauroids, banjo, adobie, poke-easy, blab, procreant, soul, crotch, hieroglyphic, nighest, nebula, tympan, electric, belch, hog, procreant, bowels,* and *lilacs.*[5]

William Carlos Williams, in the spirit of Thoreau's "simplify, simplify," urged poets to cleanse their diction of what my students would call "flowery words," and "bring it down." And some contemporary poets have written very powerfully in a spare, gritty diction—Philip Levine, for one.[6] But teenagers' language is already "down" about as far as it can go. So early in the year I ask them to keep a section of their notebook as a "word bank," in which they can record any "juicy" word they run across, in or out of class, especially a word that they think they've never used in their own writing. Rather than concentrate entirely on exposing them to words they have to look up in the dictionary, I want to help them realize that they "know" far more words than they think to use. I also point out that, while the dictionary is a wonderful mansion with many rooms to explore, as is the thesaurus, and also the dictionaries of etymologies—where they can find a word's life story— they can acquire words more easily and permanently by hearing and seeing them in a specific context. And then by using them.

It's fun to write a journal entry on your own history as a collector and employer of words. What words do you remember from the first songs and stories you ever heard? From adult conversations—that you may have misconstrued? (I remember my parents jokingly made a habit of pronouncing *nasturtiums* as Winnie the Pooh did—*mastershalums*; I forget when I finally got straightened out on this.) Many of us have our own childhood versions of The Lord's Prayer, "The Star-Spangled Banner," and "Onward, Christian Soldiers." James Thurber has a wonderful essay in which he recounts his loss of innocence about metaphors—which as a child he had taken literally. When told the little girl next door was "crying her heart out," he had eagerly gone to look for the heart; now the world was less alive with possibility.[7] What are your favorite words—and what about the ones that make you cringe? Explore possible reasons for these gut reactions. Apart from personal associations. Try saying these words aloud. Notice what certain sounds force you to do with your face and throat—*snivel, sneer, gross, titter, slobber*. On the other hand, say *almond, silver, apricot, April, azure, translucent, murmur, crimson, lullaby*. It's not just a matter of meaning, but of mouthing.

Ask your students to write the same kind of journal piece. Then invite them to choose one or two words to "meditate" on in a second entry. How does one meditate on a word? Through saying it aloud—om, om—in order to explore its sensations; through using it in a variety of ways; investigating its other forms; looking up its history; and above all, considering what associations it holds for you. When I visited the kindergarten, I noticed how much those children loved to *count* things, so when I wrote about this, I found a poem taking shape that was a kind of meditation on the word *count*:

One Door / Six Windows to Grow On

> *Monitors for everything*
> *the chair isn't alive unless*
> *they sit in it and count legs*
> *"octopus" is the Word of the Day,*
> *"tentacles" as yet unknown but*
> *present when the dreamy-eyed*
> *boy waves his arms to call out*
> *everything reborn here in the bright*
> *mind-shaped room of the monitors*
> *counting, counting, held to account*
> *for snow days cupcakes pencils straws*
> *words and days, how many days*
> *left, how many days served, how many*
> *prefer chocolate to our word of yesterday*
> *"vanilla," tomorrow's word is*
> *"what," "What do I have in my*
> *lunch today?" she offers, she is*
> *Alexandra flag-monitor, newly five*

and still counting stars, she gets to hold
the Birthday Bear and makes him pledge
allegiance, too, though he is monitor
of nothing but fur, and too wooly-minded
to count or have flu or grandparents
or keep track of the weather,
and sits by the chalkboard waiting for
someone to complete another year
and claim his/her turn for
this unaccountable love we still count on.

It's possible to "analyze" or study words almost without knowing it, if the atmosphere is relaxed and playful. One day when I was touting the virtues of having poetic license to twist words, somewhat like Humpty Dumpty, to one's own needs, a freshman boy scoffed, "Sure, like banana's a verb or something." So some of us wrote poems in which banana became a verb, and others, with a little encouragement, got up and "bananaed" around the room. From there it's a short step to making a list of popular dances over the last few hundred years the banana, the monkey, the black bottom—and getting into the important matter of how words came into the English language at various stages in our history. You can start with indigenous (a useful word to teach) words like pumpkin and moccasin. If you're lucky enough to have a number of different languages represented in your class, perhaps students who live in bilingual households or have to switch from English to something else when they get home every day, or if you simply have students who are taking various languages, you can draw on them to help cultivate an awareness of the power of sound and connotation. You may also find yourself in a good discussion about the pros and cons of cultural assimilation; if your language isn't the dominant one in the country where you live, how does this affect your life? What would it mean to lose your language?

Another means of gathering the words you'll need for writing richer, more evocative poetry, is to steal from whatever you're reading. When we begin discussing a book in class, I like to put up mural paper, hand out colored pencils, and ask everyone to contribute some favorite words and phrases from the previous night's reading. Then, we try to heighten our awareness of their sounds, and to see whether we can detect any patterns in the writer's diction: Maybe a lot of short, gritty, practical Anglo-Saxon words? A cluster of words from one particular discipline or culture or region of the country? We stand around the mural and take turns reading words aloud, trying to watch one another for cues and keeping a steady stream of sound going, without any one person directing the performance. From the first pages of Toni Morrison's *Beloved* came this music: *venom, kettleful of chickpeas, creeping-off boys, perfunctory, slop jars, rutting, palsied, dawn-colored, chamomile, brimstone, sycamore, soughing, undulating, iron eyes, stroppin' Sabbaths, blizzard of snowdrops.*

This is one of those activities that helps build a sense of community just by forcing us to pay attention to one another. It can be a surprisingly effective ritual, rather mysterious in its power. A celebration of language. Afterward, we can steal one another's words for our own collections. I like doing this exercise also after we've read a number of poems by one poet; it makes us aware of the fact that every writer's language has its own flavor. The work of Chicano poet Jimmy Santiago Baca,[8] for example, is full of earthy, full-blooded words like *sun, heart, blood, star, knife, horse,* and it is not so different, though its effect is different, from Creek Indian Joy Harjo's vocabulary.[9]

Robert Bly has said that if you possessed only seven words, you could still make a poem, if you felt those words intensely enough. I've never tested this theory, but I have assigned students a list of ten words and challenged them to write a poem that includes all ten. This exercise pushes them to consider the various ways a word can be used—verb and noun, figuratively as well as literally. It can lead to vital discussions of how words may start out life with very *literal* meanings but gradually get to be used *figuratively* as well—perhaps when poets get hold of them, desperate to express the ineffable. Take the word *brood,* for example, or *browse.*

Your ten words should include some concrete and evocative nouns, some strong, active verbs, a few specific adjectives. The students who treat this activity as a kind of verbal jigsaw puzzle, creating a sequence of events into which the words might logically fit, fail to take advantage of those "random" workings of association which sometimes summon up an unexpected insight. For them it's just an entertaining—or frustrating—exercise in ingenuity. Others are surprised and delighted at the new voice and wisdom they suddenly acquire.

I myself had been trying all winter to write something fresh and un-Wordsworthian about the lambs at the farm up the hill. This exercise finally produced a piece that felt right, and I was surprised to find that in the process I had come up with a definition of love.

These Lambs

are pure ginger.
The air frisks them for drugs.
Something in the hay they lip?
Nuzzle and nudge. Birdflight! Snowmelt!
Hindquarters are a chance affair.
Each turd electrifying news. Suddenly
one lamb does the hula,
his face in the ewe's gray flank.
He can't even walk a straight line to the barn.
Life's a scribble, a fugue for tail
and feet. This is falling in love.
When your body's architecture
goes unfamiliar. You stagger,
and howl to the circling stars,
"Enough!" You are all
doors, which open and close without
your knowing why.

No, *turd* was not on the list—just a word I'd never used in a poem before and suddenly remembered I wanted to. But *ginger, lip, chance, electric, gray, straight, architecture, enough, close,* and *suddenly* were. Try your own list and poem. Or, if you want a prescribed list, Rita Dove has one in a useful collection of poet/teachers' exercises called *The Practice of Poetry*.[10]

Next fall I'm resolved to master the Internet and set up correspondence and poetry exchanges between my students and student writers from different regions of the country and of different ethnic backgrounds. In addition to broadening everyone's outlook, it might also expand their vocabulary. The more enthusiasm we create for language, the less likely our students are to complain that poets are out to give them a hard time by using words unknown to the human ear or using them in unfair, tricky ways that conceal the meaning from all but the guy who writes the footnotes. Or, of course, the teacher, who has the answers.

In addition to collecting words from a wide range of sources, we can help students rediscover words through free-association and improvisation. If you get a beat going by chanting a few repetitive lines, you can get students to improvise *more* lines, with words that are stimulated by rhymes, rhythm, and other associations.

I started a class by reading aloud surrealist André Breton's sensuous love poem "My Woman": "My woman with her forest-fire hair / With her heat-lightning thoughts / With her hourglass waist / My woman with her otter waist in the tiger's mouth / My woman with her rosette mouth a bouquet of stars of the greatest magnitude / With her teeth of white mouse footprints on the white earth;"[11] then some of Whitman's powerful chanting—"Earth of the slumbering and liquid trees! / Earth of departed sunset—earth of the mountains misty-topt! / Earth of the vitreous pour of the full moon just tinged with blue!";[12] and some of Anne Waldman's performance poem "Fast Speaking Woman": I'm the rippling woman / I'm the gutted woman / I'm the woman with wounds / I'm the woman with shins / I'm the bruised woman / I'm the eroding woman / I'm the suspended woman / I'm the woman alluring / I'm the architect woman / I'm the trout woman / I'm the tungsten woman / I'm the woman with the keys / I'm the woman with the glue . . . ."[13] I let myself move to the rhythms.

Then I suggested that, before we tried our own chants as men and women, we make a collaborative chant on the theme of Elephant. "I'll write the lines up on the board as you shout them at me. I'll line out three possible rhythms you can use. Let's lay down a groove we can come back to whenever we want: I'm a jazz elephant. I'm a zip elephant. I'm a . . ." A kid said, hesitantly, "I'm a zapped elephant?"

"Fine! Now let's add a rhythm where you can use *two- or three-syllable-descriptions*—like I'm a razzmatazz elephant, I'm a string bass elephant, I'm an in-your-face elephant. And then for a third pattern, let's add a *phrase or clause* to the elephant—you know, like I'm an elephant with baggy knees, I'm an elephant full of fleas—or I'm an elephant who can't cope, I'm an elephant who's seen the Pope." (A quick lesson in grammar here.) They caught on, and the elephant chant grew apace. This wasn't a lesson in new words so much as juxtaposing words they didn't normally expect to see together. In a "serious" poem, some of the rhymes would have sounded forced, but here we could take advantage of the associative power of rhyme without worrying about making sense, and also explore off-rhyme. Then I sent them off to write chants of their own.

One boy celebrated the qualities he got teased about—his "feminine" side. One girl, a powerhouse on the softball team but very uncertain of her abilities as a poet, wrote:

I called for the beat
I called for the courage
I called it Amen
I called it power
I called for the loss
I called for the colors
I called for the bulls raging
I called for the sword
I called for the clown
I called for the kisses
I called for the dust
I called it a Ferris wheel
I called it depth

Chanting these aloud the next day proved to be exhilarating. I'd asked students the night before to give themselves a good fifteen minutes for chanting aloud, real improvisation, to see where the associations produced by rhythm and rhyme could take them. Then they could write down the parts they liked best, and rearrange as much as they wanted. (That weekend I found myself jazzing quietly through Penn Station to my own groove: "I'm the musk woman, I'm the sub-fusc woman, I'm the woman with the mask, I'm the woman who just can't ask, I'm the outerbanks woman, I'm the Weetabix woman. . . .")

Finally, it's very important to make time to work with the *connotation* of words. This is a tricky business, because we each bring our own religion, family traditions, knowledge of history, and experience with literature—or lack of all these—to our encounter with words. *Garden* may, for many of us, connote Eden, innocence and its loss; for us the word may call up a powerful myth that affects the way we think about human nature. For others it may connote hard work. For still others, seclusion and security. Less and less can we rely, as poets and readers of poetry, on a common body of knowledge that will reverberate to certain evocative words.

Despite cultural differences, I think we can rely on the *senses* to respond in a specific way to certain words—to tighten up or relax, to feel weighted or lightened. When I asked the seniors to write a poem about their minds, one boy came up with a list of images—interestingly contradictory ones, that capture his sense of the mind's complexity. This is a boy who, as part of his senior fourth-quarter project, drove all over New Jersey writing poems about the various towns where he stopped. He's a fine classical drummer and fascinated by Eastern religions, philosophy, and science. His words come from many different "worlds." See what associations they have for you: *rods and cones and flashing arrows, soaring birds and jagged glass, a nursing calf and the slasher from that generic B-movie, an arrow past the horizontal sunrise, a race riot, the sketched trajectory of the latest rocket to God, downward stairwells and cartoon steam valves.*

One of my favorite books, Gaston Bachelard's *The Poetics of Space,* investigates the way various kinds of space attract and concentrate the poetic imagination. Bachelard examines images of "intimacy and immensity"— *cellar and attic, drawers, chest, wardrobes, nests and shells.*[14] These are all interesting words for us and our students to write about—to see what associations, what power, they hold. I remember once taking a course in art appreciation, in which all ten of us were piloted along a row of paintings at the Museum of Modern Art and were asked to spend some time looking at the same one, making notes on what we saw and how it made us feel. As we discussed our responses, we found that there were certain areas of agreement, certain assumptions that we *all* made. This may have been in part because we were all interested in art, all from the same part of the country, all school teachers, and all women. But there were many other differences among us—age, ethnicity, religion, etc. If you give your whole class one word—"nest," for example, and ask them to write about the associations and feelings it holds for them, you will probably see certain commonalities emerge. After I do this exercise, I like to give students a whole list of evocative words that have resonated for lyric poets over the centuries, and let them choose one to write about—*garden, window, shell, door, curtain, forest, dust, water, flame.* This kind of meditation often leads to writing poems, even if I don't suggest it.

Reading and writing poetry can awaken students to the liveness of words as nothing else does. And as language comes alive for us, we find we can put our experiences into words that will touch others, that will reach, as Galway Kinnell says, "that level in the psyche where we're all the same."

Notes

1. Quincy Troupe, *Weather Reports: New and Selected Poems* (New York: Writers & Readers, 1996). See also the remarkable sequences with Troupe reading and giving workshops to prisoners in Sing Sing and to high school students on the video series *The Power of the Word* (see note 1, chap. 1).

2. Pattiann Rogers, *Splitting and Binding* (Middletown, CT: Wesleyan University Press, 1989). While there is also a *Selected Poems* available, this earlier book is one of my favorites, containing "The Family Is All There Is" and the ebullient "Rolling Naked in the Morning Dew."

3. Alice Fulton, *Sensual Math* (New York: W. W. Norton, 1995).
Fulton's language and imagery range from the scientific to the sexy.

4. A. R. Ammons, *Collected Poems 1951–1971* (New York: W. W. Norton, 1972). Ammons is a rewarding poet to read along with Frost, especially for students who not only like the outdoors and the natural sciences but are beginning to ponder how the mind works and the nature of fate and free will. Students who can listen may appreciate his quiet irony and humor.

5. Walt Whitman, *Leaves of Grass* (New York: Random House, 1993). I like to photocopy excerpts from "Song of Myself" and have my students make lists of words that they would never think to use in a poem, either because the words are unfamiliar or "just don't seem poetic." Eventually we write a Whitman-style poem, using some of these words. I also show students my very handy pocket-sized selection of Whitman's work, chosen and introduced by Galway Kinnell, *The Essential Whitman* (Hopewell, NJ: The Ecco Press, 1987). They need to get the habit of sticking small books in their pockets.

6. Philip Levine, *New Selected Poems* (New York: Knopf, 1992). I've found his collection *What Work Is* (National Book Award 1991) particularly accessible, full of tough but compassionate portraits of firefighters, factory workers, a

schoolroom full of the children of factory workers. There is also a poem that begins, "The first time I drank gin / I thought it must be hair tonic." (New York: Knopf, 1991).

7. James Thurber, "The Secret Life of James Thurber," in *The Thurber Carnival* (New York: Harper & Bros., 1945) 30.

8. Jimmy Santiago Baca, *Black Mesa Poems* (New York: New Directions, 1989). Many of my juniors and seniors have also loved Baca's powerful memoir, *Working in the Dark, Reflections of a Poet of the Barrio* (Santa Fe, NM: Red Crane Books, 1992), which begins with how he taught himself to read and write poetry in jail. And they also enjoy the sequences with Baca on "Swirl Like a Leaf," the sixth program in PBS's second poetry series, *The Language of Life*, with Bill Moyers (writ. James Haba and Richard Kelso, 1995). This eight-part video series, filmed at the 1994 Geraldine R. Dodge Poetry festival in Waterloo Village, New Jersey, comes with a teacher's guide that contains posters of all the poets, each including a photograph, three or four poems that are heard in the series, a brief bio, a few questions to think about, and several writing activities. Poets in this series: Sekou Sundiata and Naomi Shihab Nye; Coleman Barks (translator of the popular 13th-century mystic poet Jelaluddin Rumi); Linda McCarriston and Sandra McPherson; Robert Hass, Claribel Alegría, and Carolyn Forché; Gary Snyder and Daisy Zamora; Baca, Marilyn Chin, and Robert Bly; Adrienne Rich, Victor Hernández Cruz, and Michael Harper; Lucille Clifton and David Mura. For information call 1-800-257-5126 or 609-275-1400. Each program runs about an hour.

Also available now is the three-hour video made from the 1996 Dodge Festival, *Poetry Heaven*, which comes with a teacher's guide that follows a similar format but also includes a list of books for building a core high school poetry collection and one panel/conversation card offering highlights of and questions about the series' four panel discussions: Women and Poetry, Poetry and History, Poetry and Work, and A Shared Life of Poetry (with husband and wife poets Robert Hass and Brenda Hillman). The program ends with some of the Festival poets giving advice to high school poets on Student Day (the opening day of the Festival) and readings by four of the twenty student winners of the annual New Jersey state poetry contest sponsored by Dodge and/ Rutgers/Newark. *Poetry Heaven* includes a wonderful range of poets: besides Hass and Hillman (in order of appearance), Mark Doty, Thylias Moss, Pattiann Rogers, Carol Muske, Gerald Stern, Yehuda Amichai, Allen Ginsberg, Le Thi Diem Thuy, Li-Young Lee, Marie Howe, Yusef Komunyakaa, Louis Jenkins, Hal Sirowitz, Philip Levine, Joy Harjo, Robert Creeley, and Jean Valentine.

The listing in the teacher's guide provides a grid of timed locations for the poems and panel/conversations on the video. The show was offered in the spring of 1998 by satellite to PBS stations nationwide, and teachers have the right to tape and use it for one year after broadcast. To order videocassettes, contact Films for the Humanities and Sciences at 1-800-257-5126. You can order extra copies of the teacher's guide by writing to POETRY HEAVEN, Teacher's Guide, P.O. Box 245, Little Falls, NJ 07424-0245. For information about the Festival, which is held every other year in late September, visit the website at www.grdodge.org/poetry or write Poetry Festival, Geraldine R. Dodge Foundation, 163 Madison Ave., P.O.B. 1239, Morristown, NJ 07962-1239. A four-day festival, the opening Thursday is designed for students, and the poets give workshops, panel discussions, and readings especially geared to high schoolers. The second day is specifically for teachers, with the same mix of activities. Saturday and Sunday, and all four evenings, are for the general public.

9. Joy Harjo, *She Had Some Horses* (New York: Thunder's Mouth Press, 1990). Joy Harjo may be seen on PBS's first poetry series, *The Power of the Word* (see note 1, chap. 1).

10. Robin Behn and Chase Twitchell, eds., *The Practice of Poetry. Writing Exercises from Poets Who Teach* (New York: HarperCollins, 1992). This is a very useful collection of exercises by many different poet/teachers, geared toward college creative writing courses but many quite usable with high school students. They include work with the unconscious, with metaphor and image, voice, form, sound, the line, and revision.

11. André Breton, *Earthlight*, trans. Bill Zavatsky and Zack Rogow (Los Angeles: Sun & Moon Press, 1993).

12. Whitman, *Leaves of Grass* 60–61.

13. Anne Waldman, *Fast Speaking Woman* (San Francisco: City Lights Books, 1975) 3–5.

14. Gaston Bachelard, *The Poetics of Space*, trans. Maria Jolas (Boston: Beacon Press, 1969). A most unusual book that makes one want to start writing poetry right away though much of it is too difficult for most high school students. Bachelard explores certain kinds of spaces that attract the poetic imagination—nests, shells, cellars, closets—and how images arise in the individual

consciousness. I have let students choose one of these spaces, free-associate on it, consider how it affects their senses, and write a poem that grows out of these exercises. Exploring the sounds and associations of "nest" has worked especially well.

Chapter 10

Memory

*A*LL STORIES / ADD UP TO WHERE YOU ARE NOW.

WILLIAM STAFFORD, *"PRETTY GOOD DAY"*
IN *EVEN IN QUIET PLACES*

*O*ne powerful source of inspiration for poetry that we all share is our childhood. But it can be a difficult place to get back to. When my teenage students collaborate on writing projects with third or fourth graders, the older students are often too nervous to enjoy the initial stages. "What can I talk about? What will they want to write about?" I had much the same fears when I started giving workshops to elementary school children.

When I ask eleventh graders, "Well, don't you remember what it was like to be eight or nine years old?" they say, "Yeah, well, it was great. No college applications, no essay tests, no College Boards, no hunts for summer jobs—it was all fun. We were so *free* back then." There seems to be a generic, carefree childhood to which we all want to subscribe, a lost Eden. But armed with the poet's image-making powers and attentiveness to physical sensation and words, we should be able to recapture something more specifically ours.

> What is the earliest place you can remember?
> What is the first sensation you associate with school?
> When was the first time you were afraid?

When I was four—was my oldest brother born then?—we moved from a cottage on some rich family's estate to a not-quite-finished house closer to town. All I remember of the cottage is a green door in the garden wall, rabbits at twilight, and walks along a road fringed with yellow daisies whose black centers frightened me. The new house smelled of fresh paint and wood shavings, and I think maybe we visited before all the flooring had been laid down. I see mattresses on the floor, but that could have been the new cabin in Maine, four years later. Of nursery school and kindergarten I recall only the daily walk to get there, holding my mother's hand, the crackers and juice and nap times, and the fear. Fear that made me throw up on my blue gingham dress. What I was afraid of hovers somewhere out beyond the dark borders of memory. But I know it was associated with school. My own yard was scary, too, because of the fuzzy buzzing things in the clover and the possibility of a large dog with lots of teeth wandering through from next door. There was a book on my bedroom shelf with one page that I made my grandmother turn very fast so I wouldn't have to look. It had a picture of a large, black pansy right in the center that I didn't want to dream about. At night the tiny light I was allowed to have burning on my dresser helped keep the pansy and the witches away, but closing my eyes was dangerous. If I fell asleep, they would fly into my dreams. The darkness behind my eyes drew them.

Remembering even these few sensations took some effort. To remember the blue gingham dress I closed my eyes and opened the door to my bedroom closet, trying to see what dresses hung there. But I think what surfaced first was the smell of vomit on the crisply ironed cotton, and the feeling of humiliation—not the row of dresses, simply because when I was that young it was my mother, not I, who opened closets and dressers to lay out my clothes.

So rather than ask my students to summon up a house or lawn or room, I like to push them to explore the childhood sensations for which they've expressed the most nostalgia—the sense of freedom and play. And the other side of the coin—their memories of fear, helplessness, confusion.

What worries and questions would adults not answer, or at least not in ways a child could understand? What was it like to feel small or to have no control over what food you got to eat or who picked you up and kissed you? What can you remember wanting badly and being refused? What did you look forward to the most each day? What did you dread? Were you ever punished for something you didn't do? Why did you adore one baby-sitter and loathe another? What was your first encounter with an animal? Your favorite picture in a book—and how did it feel as that page was about to be turned? Did you have a secret place? A secret wish? Were you sung to or danced with, and what did that feel like? Do you remember ever getting dizzy, or going very fast? What did going to bed feel like? What is the first time you can remember feeling alone?

You might want to invite students to bring in books they loved as children, and sit on the floor to hear one another read aloud. Look at the pictures, too. Encourage everyone to try to remember what they liked so much about their book and how they feel about it now. Would they read it to *their* children? I like to read aloud from the first chapter of James Joyce's *Portrait of the Artist as a Young Man*, to show the class how well Joyce (poet as well as novelist) captured a child's vivid physical sensations of helplessness and fear, his sense of wonder, and his distortions and misreadings of what, by adults, is taken for granted[1]:

> When you wet the bed, first it is warm then it gets cold. His mother put on the oilsheet. That had the queer smell.
>
> His mother had a nicer smell than his father. She played on the piano the sailor's hornpipe for him to dance. . . .
>
> Uncle Charles and Dante [his aunt] clapped . . . Dante gave him a cachou every time he brought her a piece of tissue paper.
>
> The Vances lived in number seven. They had a different father and mother. They were Eileen's father and mother. When they were grown up he was going to marry Eileen. He hid under the table. His mother said:

—O, Stephen will apologise.

Dante said:

O, if not, the eagles will come and pull out his eyes—
Pull out his eyes.—
Apologise,
Apologise,
Pull out his eyes.

One of my freshmen boys surprised me by admitting that the first sensation he remembered was being held in his mother's lap:

I remember you cuddling me
when I took my naps
or you dozing while I
ever
so
slowly
tried to get up and go play.
You always hugged me,
dragging me back to safety
just as one foot touched the floor.

The day we each brought in a favorite toy—mostly stuffed animals—and talked about what had been so special about it, a freshman girl wrote about her teddy bear, focusing on its eyes:

I think they can see inside,
those shining clear glass eyes
the only ones
that were always on my side.
And after nightmares
their golden glints
scared the monsters away.

Even if I tossed those eyes
into the laundry hamper,
they always forgave me

and still wait for me on my bed.

When we investigated children's poetry—from our own bookshelves but also through an exchange of letters and poems with our third-grade pen pals, we found that children love poems that rhymed, and also love reading and writing about food. This brought up a lot of memories. "Wouldn't it be great to be able to eat all you wanted and not worry about gaining weight!" one freshman girl sighed. "Yeah, but I never got enough when I was a kid. Now at least we can buy our own pizza and we're big enough to reach the freezer door," a boy reminded her. "But now we know what's healthy and what's junk. I wish I didn't know." This was the girl who wrote my favorite of the class poems about food. Her ending reminded me of the times I used to get excused from the table to go to the bathroom and would carefully flush away pieces of meat I'd patiently stashed in the back of my mouth; I remember being scared they were too big to slide down my throat.

For afternoon snacks
I'd have a few crackerjacks,
four chocolate eclairs,
nine creamsicle pops
Then mother declared
the sweets were to stop
So in came the peas,
the broccoli trees,
two celery sticks
and vegetable mix,
zucchini in slices
with multi-grain rices,
romaine lettuce head
on a slice of wheat bread,
some freshly baked trout

topped with cold sauerkraut,
hot oatmeal in season
and bran without reason.

My plate was infested
just as mom planned,
but to say I digested,
well, the dog had a hand.

Notice how rhyming led her to the wonderful image of her plate being "infested" with healthful food. If this childhood Eden of four eclairs in one afternoon is too good to last, at least the child is putting up some heroic resistance.

One day I read aloud from Dylan Thomas's "Fern Hill", asking the class to experience with their senses the intensity of color and light and motion in this vision of childhood[2]:

     Time let me hail and climb

   Golden in the heydays of his eyes,
And honoured among wagons I was prince of the apple towns
And once below a time I lordly had the trees and leaves
    Trail with daisies and barley
   Down the rivers of the windfall light.

  . . . .

All the sun long it was running, it was lovely, the hay
Fields high as the house, the tunes from the chimneys, it was air
   And playing, lovely and watery
    And fire green as grass.

I stopped there. "Of course, this couldn't last," a girl said. "No, but he was able to remember it," her friend suggested. "He was lucky to have that to remember. He was lucky to find the words to remember it that way." We talked about the sounds and some of the surprising phrases—"once below a time," "rivers of the windfall light," "all the sun long," and "fire green as grass." We agreed that these phrases made the child's world seem full of possibility, beyond the limits of time and space and ordinary logic.

"Why don't you try creating a world in which you, the child, are 'prince of the apple towns.' See what colors and motion and word play and impossibilities your imagination creates."

As I walked around the room, students were already jotting down lines. A few were making sketches. A couple were humming quietly. Quite a number had found a corner on the floor or were perched on the window ledge. I was curious what Romi would write. His poems so far had reflected a strong penchant for surrealism and political anarchy and tended to be very full of abstract nouns. Also extremely long. Childhood hadn't interested him particularly. Four years later, he would end up at the University of Chicago, studying philosophy and politics. But this assignment apparently allowed the playful side of anarchy and surrealism an outlet!

> As purple giraffes kiss the night sky,
> flying into the heavens,
> the rain falls gently on fields of violets,
> the grass grows like spaghetti in the air and
> dances with the smiling trees.
> We all see the monkey in the monkey bars,
> and the jungle gym is wild,
> the children are painting the teacher invisible.
> All I think about are eyeballs bouncing up and
> down like basketballs.
> I hang on the ground and don't hear any sounds.
> All I hear is me breathing and the
> fluttery wings of a peacock.
> In the cold, the clouds are a warm blanket
> for the world, in the heat
> the moon will illuminate us with its cold light,
> and there is no tomorrow.
> We can play forever and ever.

Snapshots are helpful in triggering memories, and sharing family pictures can help a class develop a sense of community very fast. I asked everyone to bring in pictures of themselves as children, engaged in some activity or in a specific place that might generate memories, or in a family group. We shared our pictures, asking questions, pointing out impressions. Often the group's questions helped us remember more details. Some people began writing prose description, to see where that would take them, while some plunged right into a poem. One girl's snapshot marked an important move her family made when she was seven, from New Orleans to New Jersey. Looking at the picture, she wrote:

> This is a day of transition—a day I was wishing had never come. I am clutching onto the first seven years of my life, as hard as I can. I can feel the swelling of my eyes as the tears make their way out. I have every right to cry, to moan, to yell. I think that if I can only cry loud enough, we will not have to move. I want them to feel guilty for bringing this upon me. I want them to hurt like I hurt.
>
> My mom had promised me that we would never move. I remember the promise so clearly. It was while she was blowing my hair dry. . . . Andrew just stands there, looking pretty, without any visible notion of the circumstances. He simply is going with the flow. But in his innocent look there is the potential for pain which he will come to feel. I suppose it is the stories that we're to tell him—stories of our short but formative time there together. Or perhaps it will be the pictures we show Andrew which will remind him he used to belong to a wonderful place for the first four years of his life that he cannot fully find in his memories.
>
> . . . .
>
> A couple of days before this picture was taken, it rained. The sky let its juices out. My dad and I were on our way to Mandina's, to get me a snowcone. He took my hand and as we began to dance, he exclaimed, "Feel the rain—let it pour on you—let yourself get wet." With every drop of rain that hit me, I felt more alive. For those few seconds, nothing mattered. This was my last memory of Louisiana before the move.

This prose piece handles time shifts remarkably well. But transferring such complexity to a poem proved to be more difficult for Katherine. The poem that emerged from these memories focused on the snowcone; she enjoyed spelling out the finer points of this delicacy for her Northern friends, and ended up with a poem that is sensuous, playful, and slightly satirical—as well as nostalgic:

Snowcone

> God what would I do for a snowcone?
> To return again—
> to translucent memories
> of a place where people
> devour small red monsters
> called crawfish—the best part
> being the juicy heads and
> the feeling of satisfaction afterwards
> that you had a "good one".
> A horde of fat cajuns sitting around
> slurping Dixie beer,
> consuming each other
> spice trickling down their fingers.
> A feeling of communion
> Oh, but a snowcone. . . .
> What fluff—pure scintillation.
> A slurpee could never compete.
> The true problem
> is picking the best flavor.
> Today, Tiger's Blood sounds lovely,
> yesterday I chose Grape.
> Greasy pleasure.
> I let it out—libre.
> And they say
> "Pass A Good Time Chere."

Revisiting the past can feel strange if you haven't made a habit of it. It's like buried treasure. You can't remember exactly where you left the chest, so you need a map. As I write this, I realize this hidden chest is an image I've used at least twice in my own poems. One was to Chris, a close friend whose father had abandoned the family when he (Chris) was still a child:

> You distrust warm beds
> and a lantern swaying in the night.
> You keep returning to your runaway father—

an empty treasure chest.
What prayers does it take to release a ghost
to a new history and weather?

To return—through dark woods or over storm-gray waves—to search,
perhaps in vain, at the foot of a tree: In writing about the quest for your
childhood, you almost inevitably wander into myth. Roots of a magic tree,
chests, swords, chalices, caves, closets, crossroads, river crossings, gardens,
the music of birds and harps or of your own pounding heart. The fear of
darkness but the mysterious, tantalizing, even reassuring sensation of
having passed this way before: This quest is like trying to reenter a dream
you can't quite forget. Those are the dreams that haunt you till you write
about them, a process which is a kind of quest or entering. I once wrote a
poem about a child who came for me in a dream:

"I don't speak the language of your country,"
you said, and somehow I understood.
Was it the icy air that gave your tongue
clarity? Or those keen hills?
"Cavaross," you said, and the word froze in mid-air.
I could hold it in my hand. "Sled,"
and we were sliding fast between hills,
you a small boy, innocent eyes, fur—
were you part animal?—snugged in my lap
so tight that no lurch around a corner
spun you out. You quivered through my thick wool,
"I love your country." And the hills hurled snow
into your outstretched arms, as we skimmed,
no sled now, just our bodies fused,
smoothing the icy humps that reared
sudden as separation. "Why are you here?"
My thought was a white hare frozen alive, but you knew.
Confiding hands took mine.
"A king sent for me," you said, "and now
I want to stay. Please ask him. Please?" You
didn't know his name, how could I ask?
Oh come back, press your cold face against mine.

"Cavaross," I say to the dying
tongues that mutter in the grate.
Come back and call snow from the hills.

Of course the suppression of certain kinds of memories is entirely understandable. A number of times I have been struck by the courage of my student writers to probe an experience that they might well be forgiven for leaving strictly alone.

One day a junior girl came to me to confer about a paper she'd turned in uncompleted. "Well, how do you feel about the part you've written so far," I asked. The essay was in response to a disturbing poem by Yusef Komunyakaa—"My Father's Love Letters"—in which a son recounts how his illiterate and abusive father made him write letters to his mother, begging her to return home. "He would beg, / Promising to never beat her / Again. Somehow I was happy / She had gone. . . ."[3] The girl—I'll call her Becky— looked uncomfortable. "Well, it's a poem about, you know, abuse. And I've kind of, like, been through it. So I don't really want to read about it."

We tried to sort this out. Yes, it happened a while back. No, it wasn't still going on. Yes, of course she could write on a different poem. "Maybe I shouldn't have assigned this poem at all." "Well," said Becky, "I guess kids need to know about it. I mean, people think this stuff only happens in movies or big cities." It turned out that she'd been writing poems for many years and was interested in having me read one. Next day I found it on my desk.

Every time I pass the bathroom door
my eyes are drawn to
the tiny rusted hook and eye
mounted
to where a mezuzah should hang.
I feel revolutions of my tears
drowning me out.
The strong vibrations of my father's voice,
"I'm going to have to lock you in the bathroom again,"
churn through my dreams.
Because I know it's not over.
The friction of my legs dragging

along the green woolen carpet
as he pulls me by my arm with a forceful grip—
left his thumbprints.
I feel his knees digging into the small of my back
torturing my fragile bones
as my mother looks on.
But it doesn't hurt,
I won't cry—
my body, stripped of all dignity,
because he knows too much
and he's got my mouth
beneath his securely cupped hand—always.

And he cries—
makes me feel guilty
as if I forced him to act this way.
And then his routine apology,
I have memorized word for word,
floats above my head
'cause I refuse to let him hurt me.

The old battered cement wall
that has been my companion
is now a gift to my baby brother.
I try to protect him, shield him from the hate,
but I know he has to make his own wall—
mine is all used up.

Becky said that writing poems had helped her get through those years, although she also, eventually, got professional help. I think this is one of those cases in which poetry served as a useful adjunct to therapy, but I wouldn't discount the strengths of the poem for this reason. I watched its author take my criticisms—more than I could have done at her age, on so personal a poem. I watched her come up with suggestions for tightening, for cutting out some of the unnecessary explanation of her feelings and letting concrete details do the work. As we talked, she made it clear that she wanted to know whether the poem would speak to other students, so we agreed that I would use it, anonymously, with my freshmen in a discussion I was planning about the places they might turn for help with various kinds of personal problems—academics, pregnancy, alcoholism, divorced parents, suicidal friends, harassment, abuse.

It made a big impact on the ninth-graders. They'd never read a student poem on abuse; many said they'd never imagined students "at this school" having such an experience. They admired the nameless writer's courage and said that the poem made it easier for them to talk about all the issues we brought up that day.

There are things one can never know about oneself—roots that are untraceable, water whose depths can't be taken—but the act of creating art will often bring up drowned or buried treasure. "Those are pearls that were his eyes." To live so entirely in the present and immediate future, as many of my older students seem to do, isn't possible; the past has a powerful hold on us. But even to *try* to do this is impoverishing, if not destructive. Watching juniors and seniors focus so single-mindedly on getting into college, I feel as though they are walling themselves into a very narrow, suffocating space. To look back can sometimes be very painful, but how else can we see ourselves as organic, as growing?

It's not a matter of studying our past in order to assign blame and praise and then file the memories away, but rather to sense, I think, that there has been movement and may be more—that we have this vital capacity to keep growing. Poetry can be a means of discovering and commemorating this vitality.

Notes

1. James Joyce, *A Portrait of the Artist as a Young Man* (New York: Viking, 1976) 8.

2. Dylan Thomas, "Fern Hill" in *The Collected Poems* (New York: New Directions, 1957) 178–180.

3. Yusef Komunyakaa, "My Father's Love Letters" in *Magic City* (Hanover, NH: Wesleyan University Press/University Press of New England, 1992) 43. This is a poem, along with "Venus's-flytraps" from the same collection, that I have used repeatedly with students at various schools. Komunyakaa's Vietnam poems are also very accessible—one of my students' favorites is "Facing

It," about the Vietnam Memorial—and may be found, along with some good poems on jazz, in Komunyakaa's Pulitzer Prize-winning *Neon Vernacular: New and Selected Poems* (Hanover, NH: University Press of New England, 1993).

Chapter 11

Finding Your Poet

I'LL LET THEM READ WHAT THEY WISH. AND THEN WE'LL HAVE SOME FUN IN THEIR TELLING ME WHY THEY MADE THEIR CHOICE; WHY A THING CALLED TO THEM.

ROBERT FROST, INTERVIEW WITH ROSE C. FELD

Can you remember the first time you fell in love with a writer? Maybe it was the Christmas you were given the Narnia books? Or your first Dr. Seuss? Can you remember devouring all of Sherlock Holmes or *The Count of Monte Cristo* or the Tolkien trilogy under the blankets with a flashlight? And then came the summers on the road with Kerouac, and the Hemingway year of the locked jaw, when everything was fine and good and true, and the beach summer of *Gone with the Wind*. And still later the white nights with Dostoevsky. And the summer hitching from hostel to hostel with those two European novels in your backpack; or swaying in the subway with Joseph Heller and Philip Roth.

I've noticed that when I ask colleagues to reminisce, they rarely mention a poet. Well, maybe Plath or Ginsberg or e. e. cummings, but only when pressed up against the wall. And I suspect this is because we were led to believe that poetry was hard work, requiring the presence of a teacher and a scalpel.

How did we discover our favorite writers? Through browsing in the attic or the library or our parents' shelves. Or, more likely, word of mouth; there were years when every kid from twelve to eighteen was reading *Catcher in the Rye.* Right now my student poets are carrying around Sharon Olds's *The Gold Cell*[1] (the girls, that is) and Ginsberg[2] and Galway Kinnell.[3]

There are so many wonderful, accessible poets "out there" right now that it's easy to find a favorite. Classroom texts are beginning to include a greater diversity of voices. But I think it's important for students to see us hold up a book of poems *we're* currently reading and flip through the pages till we find one we love: "Here, this is it. Listen, you gotta hear this one . . . !"

Browsing in the poetry shelves of a good bookstore is a delight. Several of the big chains—Encore and Borders, for instance—usually have a wide selection. You can find anthologies that focus on poets of one particular ethnic background or nationality, collections of women poets, Holocaust poets, Zen Buddhist poets, poets writing about jazz, about AIDS. You can find books of father/daughter poems, of marriage poems, of bad verse, of poems for men, of animal poems and bird poems, of poets choosing their own favorite poem, even—and I bought this one specifically with teenage boys in mind—poems about driving cars![4]

Some of these bookstores will also have literary periodicals in their magazine section. I remember falling in love with Pattiann Rogers and Marilyn Hacker when I read a couple of their poems in *Poetry Northwest* and *Poetry*, years before they started winning prizes for their books. Treat yourself some afternoon when there's no committee meeting; find a bookstore with a cafe where you can actually browse over coffee, and choose a poet to take home with you. (If you bring your notebook along, you may also get inspired to start writing a poem of your own.)

I haunt used-book sales. And libraries. Even the smallest town library can offer surprises; in the tiny village of Lovell, Maine, I found a battered collection of Native American poetry and an anthology of "best" contemporary poems selected by the Academy of American Poets.

Poetry readings and videotapes—and the occasional television interview or radio reading—offer an immediacy that students love. You can check bookstore, library, and cafe schedules for readings, consult your state or local arts council, look at the ads in *Poets and Writers* magazine or *American Poetry Review,* and, if you live near a big city, find out whether there's a monthly poetry calendar of events. Two good sources I use for audiotapes, which can be surprisingly inexpensive, are The Poetry Source, in Lawrenceville, New Jersey, and Spring Church Book Company in Spring Church, Pennsylvania.

Students like to feel they've made their own discovery, so it's important to provide a lot of different poets for them to consider. And not just the ones in the textbook, because then they get the idea that poems come ready-made for the classroom and that the single anthologized poem by Ginsberg is the only one he ever wrote. And that after writing it, he promptly dropped dead. (I know, there's no date on the page to indicate this, but it's how they think.) I like to photocopy a lot of poems, scatter them on the floor or around the walls, and let students browse till they find one they want to read to us. Or put packets together and ask everyone to go home and skim till they find a couple of poems they want to present in class the next day. This kind of assignment implies, I think, that we respect their taste, their individuality. It can give them the confidence to start trusting their own reactions to poems.

My favorite sources of taped readings and interviews are the Waterloo Festival series of videos, *Power of the Word* and *The Living Language.*[5] These were made with Bill Moyers for Public Television, and represent a wonderful range of contemporary poets reading and talking about poetry, mostly at the Geraldine R. Dodge Poetry Festivals. Poets include African American poets Rita Dove, Lucille Clifton, Quincy Troupe, and Michael Harper; Native Americans Joy Harjo and Mary TallMountain; Claribel Alegría and Daisy Zamora from Nicaragua; Victor Hernández Cruz from Puerto Rico and New York City; Chinese American Li-Young Lee; as well as Gary Snyder, Adrienne Rich, Robert Bly, Stanley Kunitz, Galway Kinnell, Robert Hass, W. S. Merwin, Sharon Olds, Carolyn Forché, and Gerald Stern. Each tape, which includes two or three poets, comes with a set of posters—that you are permitted to copy. These posters include photos, a brief biographical sketch, two or three poems by each of the poets on the tape, and some questions to think about. There is also a teachers' kit of suggested exercises and topics for discussion, put together by teacher/poets from New Jersey.

You can show brief clips from a tape and follow these with discussion or writing. I like to photocopy the two or three posters for one tape and ask students to go home and browse till they decide which poem they want to read aloud to us the next day. They practice reading it, preferably to some-one at home, till they know it well enough to "give it" to us with convic-tion—with clarity and eye contact. They also write out a few questions they'd like to ask the author.

Next day we hear these readings. Find out in advance how many dupli-cates you have, so the class doesn't end up hearing the same poem four times in a row; but it's interesting to hear the same poem by *two* successive readers, so that you can discuss the different interpretations. Later, when they hear the poet read it on the tape, they'll have a context; some may prefer the way a classmate read it. We've had arguments over interpreta-tions that have taken us deep into the poem—even to the nitty gritty of grammar: "But I think the *he* in this line refers to the father, not the kid. So that changes the way you'd have to read it. It changes the whole *meaning*." Students may find a poem becomes richer for them when they hear two different readings that both "make sense." It can be very revealing, for example, to listen to a poem read by both a male and a female voice.

It's important to establish right from the start that "giving" a poem requires effort from both reader and listener. I tell students to turn over their copies of the poems during readings and to focus all their energy on the reader. I describe how when I give readings of my own poems, I'm always looking for a responsive face or presence who will give me energy and to whom I can direct the poem. I ask the student reader to take a few breaths and gather all our eyes before starting to read. If someone gets off to a bad start, it's worth asking her to begin again. Poet/teacher John Timpane gives good advice: Read "distinctly and positively, with a little push behind the words. . . . Use your chest and throat. Speak expressively. Look for surprises and gently emphasize them. Use slight pauses as emphasis. Treat white space as time. Pause gently at the end of lines—unless it's awkward. Add pauses if the poem skips lines or if lines are indented. At the ends of lines that don't end in punctuation marks, lift your tone of voice just a little. Give a sense of expectancy, of being pulled into the next line." And—very important—"No need to rush."[6]

We want to sense that the reader cares about the poem and about passing it along to us. I also ask each student to begin by telling us why she chose this poem—and, if she likes, to specify anything she especially wants us to notice.

After the readings, you can hear some of the questions that students would like to ask their poets, and get these up on the board to create a context for the interviews they'll hear. Then show the tape—pausing if you want to hear student responses to a particular reading or issue. I always ask everyone to jot down at least three things that caught their attention—it might be a comment one of the poets made about how he or she writes, or a question Moyers asked, or the way a poet read a line, or a new aspect of a poem that emerged from the reading. Then at the end, we compare notes.

Gradually, as students hear and read more and more poems, they'll become more confident in their tastes and more able to articulate why they prefer one poet to another. Of course, their tastes may not jibe with ours. But that may be as well; our tastes were probably quite different when we were sixteen from what they are now. I didn't fully appreciate Emily Dickinson till this winter, when my mother was dying and I found myself reading certain poems over and over. I suppose it was partly the language she found for the New England birds and hills and "slants of light" that my mother loved, too; and partly the stoical spareness—not a word wasted. I read three Dickinson poems at the memorial service, and I know that whenever I encounter them again they'll bring back that time in my life. I also rediscovered an early poem by Marilyn Hacker that I had admired but now loved even more, "Rune of the Finland Woman," based on a line from Andersen's fairy tale, *The Snow Queen:* "She could bind the winds of the world in a single strand."[7] The poem works magic with its variations on this line, and pays tribute to the remarkably varied capacities of a wise woman. I read the poem to everyone I could find and at a memorial concert for my mother, as well.

The poetry text I used when I first started teaching—*Sound and Sense*— had a section of paired poems, one of which was "good" and the other not. We were supposed to train our students' taste by asking them to compare the two. Invariably my students chose the "sentimental" or "obvious" or just plain tacky one. I felt like a failure, and so did they. Taste matures, especially if you fall in love often enough. And would we really want to be without the memory of that first love?

Nowadays I take comfort from a passage in Rilke's *Letters to a Young Poet*: "Works of art are of an infinite loneliness and with nothing so little to be reached as with criticism. Only love can grasp and hold and be just toward them. Consider *yourself* and your feeling right every time with regard to every such argumentation, discussion or introduction; if you are wrong after all, the natural growth of your inner life will lead you slowly and with time to other insights. Leave to your opinions their own quiet undisturbed development, which, like all progress, must come from deep within and cannot be pressed or hurried by anything."[8]

 This advice was addressed to a nineteen-year-old who was already sensitive to literature, but I think it's relevant for any adolescent reader. Students need to experience powerful, immediate, personal encounters with art if they're to fall in love with it. I didn't appreciate Elizabeth Bishop the first time I read her. Once a student finds a poet he connects with in some way, he's much more likely to look around for others.

The most effective means I've found for helping students to discover their own poet is the Project. I first tried it in my one-semester poetry course with the juniors and seniors. It does require setting aside at least a couple weeks for reading and another couple weeks for hearing presentations, depending on the size of the class; but it's well worth the time, and can be a great climax to the year or semester. One of my more "difficult" juniors, who had just emerged from an abusive relationship with a boyfriend and was still reeling from her parents' divorce, ended up writing about the project in her final course evaluation:

> When I came into class on the first day, I sat down ready to learn about white, male, upper-class, seventeenth-century poets. I was not looking forward to this. I chose this course because I was interested in poetry and I figured I would be able to get a few good poems written and read by other people who knew something about what they were doing. Then I thought I could "b.s." my way around the poetry I believed we were going to read. . . . By the time the first class was over I wanted to call my mother to tell her all about what we were planning on doing for the rest of the semester. One of the aspects I was more than willing to get started on was discovering new poets, beat poets, recent poets, poets I could relate to. Not only did I meet a lot of poets I hadn't heard of before, I learned a lot about myself too. . . . Discovering Jane Cooper was a

meaningful experience for me.[9] We had read only a sprinkling of her work in class, and I loved her instantly. At the time we had begun thinking about who we wanted for our poetry projects, and when we heard Cooper in New York I wanted to have her for my project. When I began getting to know her work better, I realized that we had some type of connection. Through her poetry I could see some of the pain I had felt in my life. I understood her poems.

Interestingly, the variety of contemporary poets we looked at seemed to reconcile this student to struggling with Coleridge's "Rime of the Ancient Mariner"—a poem I thought would have no chance with her: "I thought I was never going to get through reading it, but once I did I wanted and had to read it again. . . . I chose to write a journal entry from the wedding guest's point of view. I retold the tale in his own words and imagined his reactions to what he had been told . . . I had never read a poem that long before."

Look around your class and ask yourself what poet *you* would choose for the boy in the back row who loves to challenge everything you say; for the girl who you happen to know is living in the shadow of her older, more glamorous sister; for the boy who did Outward Bound last summer and is head of the environmental club; for the brilliant violinist with the pushy, possessive mother; for the flamboyant actress; the avid horsewoman; the feisty feminist just back from a march in Washington.

Then consider: Allen Ginsberg, Gregory Corso,[10] or Lawrence Ferlinghetti,[11] all Beat poets who challenged the Establishment on issues ranging from nuclear war to marriage; Diane Wakoski,[12] creator of powerful images in free verse, who wrote a lot about her relation to her family and her need to find out who she was; Gary Snyder,[13] ecologist and practicing Zen Buddhist, who spent a summer in his youth on top of a mountain in a fire tower; Russell Edson,[14] poet of dark, absurdist dialogues and Freudian animal fables about thoroughly dysfunctional families; Anne Sexton,[15] playwright and poet, for whom every reading was a theatrical performance; Maxine Kumin,[16] owner of a working farm, whose poems about animals are vivid and realistic; and Marge Piercy,[17] activist and poet, who writes of the needs and natures of women. Somehow, these students and poets should be finding one another.

The Project requires each student to select a twentieth-century poet writing in English (though I once allowed a brilliant Spanish student to choose Pablo Neruda, since she could read him in Spanish), to read as widely and deeply as possible in the poems—and journals and letters, if these are available—and present a fifteen-minute reading of those poems he considers most accessible to us and most characteristic. The reading includes the student's own commentary on these poems and on the whole body of work. Research into biography and criticism is not the focus of the project, but as the students get farther into the poems, they begin to have questions about how these relate to their poet's life and, perhaps, start to wonder how the poems have been received; at this point, I encourage them to do a little research, but to share with us *only* those discoveries that will help us to appreciate the poems we'll be hearing.

I present a list of some forty or fifty poets for their consideration. I confine it to twentieth-century poets, with the emphasis on contemporary writers or at least those from the forties onward, because I want students to have their own insights and form their own opinions, not be overwhelmed by the "received" views. This means that some of their poets are so current that there is very little biographical *or* critical material available, but literary magazines offer reviews and sometimes biographical background, as do video- and audiotapes.

In addition to the oral presentations, students assemble a table of contents for a hypothetical Selected Works—some twenty poems they would choose as a representation of their poet's most interesting and accessible work. They write a three- or four-page introduction to the collection, designed to help orient potential readers unfamiliar with this poet. And, finally, they each write a poem to or about their poet, imitating his or her style.

The search for a poet to live with for this long a stretch is a valuable process, and one that engages students at a very personal level. Since I don't allow any duplication, there can be some heavy negotiating over such popular figures as Plath, Olds, Ginsberg, Joy Harjo. I hand out browsing sheets on which every student must record at least three poets he's investigated, list some poems he's read by each one, and give a reason why he would or would not want to read more. If your school library holdings are weak in contemporary poetry, send students off to the local libraries and bookstores to browse.

As soon as everyone has a poet, you may want to make at least a couple of class periods available for reading, so you can watch the process and establish some guidelines. I require that students note down their observations as they progress from poem to poem, and I give them a list of items to look for, which have become familiar from our previous reading and writing of poetry—recurring themes, words, images, forms, and attitudes—so they can begin to characterize their poet.

Shaping the oral presentation requires a lot of thought: how best to convey a poet's work to the class in such limited time? Some students choose to provide handouts for everyone—of a particularly hard poem that they think we'll not "get" just from hearing it aloud, or of an extra poem they couldn't squeeze in but "you *have* to read," or a chronology of the poet's life and work, or a photograph, or quotations from an interview. Some students start by giving us a question to think about, as a context for the reading; some begin right away with a poem. I emphasize that their mission is to interest us in their poet. They are responsible for helping us enter the world of those poems. Each student is assigned a colleague whose performance he will evaluate in writing, anonymously; I quote from that evaluation in my own assessment.

By the time the day for the first presentation arrives, students are excited. And with reason. The last few years have seen some memorable moments . . . Becca sits down crosslegged on a small rug, lights the incense, turns on a tape of Indian sitar music, and invites us to join her on the floor to listen to sections from Ginsberg's "Howl." Merritt enters in a tight, red silk dress, inserts a cigarette in a long holder, fixes us with a compelling gaze, and speaks in the first person as Anne Sexton, telling us about her therapy before she starts to read from *Wanting to Die.* In a moving presentation on Theodore Roethke,[18] Dan focuses on the poems about fathers and sons, and explains how his own relationship has developed with his brilliant writer father. David confides with engaging frankness that he has recently fallen in love and then proceeds to give a convincing rendition of some of e. e. cummings's love poems. And Peter comes in wearing a dress and babushka to read us Russell Edson's ironic, nasty little fables; he explains that he thinks of fables as being told by old women, and makes us sit on the floor around his feet as he reads. Because the men in these poems are so often denied food and sex and power by the women, he interrupts his reading to unwrap a chocolate bar and, slowly, consumes it; we sit there watching hungrily.

These marriages between reader and poet sometimes have an important impact on student writing. One year a girl wrote a poem about a father who verbally abuses his wife while the teenage daughter looks on. "Tracy" seemed very ambivalent about what degree of emotional investment she had in the poem—how she herself felt about this girl. In fact, I found her almost frighteningly detached, though I was glad she wanted to work on language and line breaks. Then she heard Linda McCarriston[19] read at the Waterloo Festival. Afterwards, McCarriston spoke about the importance of writing honestly about your feelings, no matter how frightening or ugly they might be. Gradually, Tracy began to explore her feelings in her journal. When she chose to work on Anne Sexton for her project, I wondered whether reading this Confessional poet would affect her own poetry. In her final exam essay, she focused on what she had learned from Sexton:

> This course has taught me how to use writing as a release. In the past I would write about incidents that caused me to have emotions but I could not or would not confront the emotions themselves. Through reading and learning about confessional poetry I have begun to make the connection between the heart and the brain. It has taken my writing away from the surface and plunged it deep within me. Poets like Sexton, Plath, and McCarriston have caused me to question my emotions rather than denying them until I cannot feel their presence. . . . When I wrote the poem titled "The Fall," I simply told of an event that created many powerful and difficult emotions. They were difficult because I could not handle them. One of the reasons I wrote the poem was that I was having trouble accepting these emotions. However, I didn't take the next step and explore what emotions the situation caused. . . . Before this course I could easily write as a narrator of the event, but I could not write as a narrator of my soul. . . . For the first time I wrote a poem in first person this past month. Through writing this way I have learned things about myself that I have never looked for before. I am no longer just retelling my tale. I am folding inward and exploring what there is to find.

Once in a while, I think a writer arrives in our life just at the moment when we most need her. There was a senior girl in my class last year who had been hospitalized very recently for manic-depression. She had tried to kill herself and was still confused and unhappy, but was being released and sent back to school on anti-depressants. I had once heard the poet Jane Kenyon read a very powerful poem about the history of her own lifelong clinical depression, "Having It Out with Melancholy," and as I watched my student sitting in poetry class day after day, totally numbed to her own feelings by medication and unable to write, I suddenly remembered Kenyon's poem.[20] Since "Carol" later chose to write an essay on her encounter with this poem, I'll let her tell the story:

> Poetry saved my life, barely. This may sound like an overstatement, but it isn't.
>
> I have always expressed myself through poetry, but I never realized the incredible healing powers poetry had on my soul. It's so easy to pick up a pen and write down all of the horrible, or wonderful, emotions building up inside. This year, however, I became overwhelmed by the awful and found that it drained too much energy to sleep, let alone write. My body worked on automatic pilot. I was experiencing so many emotions that being alive became a chore. I've always hated doing chores. I decided to stop living. Inside, I had died long before I took those pills.
>
> After a brief vacation from everything that upset me, I had to return to school. The halls were so blurry I couldn't focus on conversations, people's faces. My surroundings were hostile and unwelcoming. How could I return to a life that became so unbearable I had to escape from it? Didn't my parents know that school was killing me all over again? Questions like those were like gusts of helium filling a red balloon. I was once again removed from my life. I floated above, with my senses dulled, and was quite content— up high and numb.
>
> When some of the helium was removed from my head, I began to complete assignments. One in particular was a political poem. The poem was entitled 'Manic Mad.' It consisted of complaints which I had about the lifeless, broken person I was nurturing inside my mind, heart, and blood. A few days later, Ms. Michaels gave me a life preserver. It was a beautiful, touching book by Jane Kenyon called *Constance*. As I read Kenyon's poems (especially 'Having It Out with Melancholy'), there was an instant connection. I was not alone, and every time I read the line 'Unholy ghost you are certain to come again' my vision gradually got clearer. Jane Kenyon had written all of the feelings I was too afraid to release. I believed there was safety in my madness. It was a cave I could crawl into whenever I felt threatened.
>
> I do not know whether my receiving that book was an act of God or just the instincts of a teacher. My loneliness and confusion are

diminishing everyday, due to *Constance*. I did not feel joy in Jane Kenyon's sorrow. I felt a comforting shelter in the knowledge that others often experience what I have. I do not know what I would have written about if I never read that book. I do not know if I would be here.

Notes

1. Sharon Olds, *The Gold Cell* (New York: Knopf, 1987). This is a collection girls read aloud to one another. Olds writes frankly, in vividly kinesthetic images, about sex, love, loss, having and raising children, and—very important to adolescent girls—a daughter's confusing relationship with her father. This is my favorite of her books. But it's only fair to admit that some parents and administrators and colleagues might be troubled by some of the material. Olds reads and talks with Bill Moyers on the video of the first PBS series, *The Power of the Word* (see note 1, chap. 1 and note 9, chap. 9).

2. Allen Ginsberg, *Collected Poems 1947–1980* (New York: Harper & Row, 1984). Students can love the rebelliousness and jazziness and humor of Ginsberg without getting any of the historical references. Alas. Kenneth Koch, in *Sleeping on the Wing* (see note 9, chap. 3) has a small cluster of Ginsberg excerpts (a little bit from "Howl" and some shorter poems along with a helpful writing exercise). Some school libraries won't touch Ginsberg, I've been told by students at schools I've visited, so you may have to photocopy or read aloud or play tapes.

3. Kinnell (see note 4, chap. 4 and note 1, chap. 1) .

4. Some examples of anthologies on themes listed in this chapter:

Michael Harper and Anthony Walton, eds., *Every Shut Eye Ain't Asleep: An Anthology of Poetry by African Americans Since 1945* (New York: Little, Brown and Co., 1994).

Duane Niatume, ed., *Harper's Anthology of 20th Century Native American Poetry* (New York: Harper & Row, 1988).

Garrett Hongo, ed. *The Open Boat: Poems from Asian America* (New York: Anchor Books, 1993).

Ray Gonzalez, ed. *After Atzlan: Latino Poets of the Nineties* (Boston: David R. Godine, 1992).

Florence Howe, ed., *No More Masks! An Anthology of Twentieth-Century American Women Poets* (New York: HarperCollins, 1993).

Jane Hirshfield, ed., *Women in Praise of the Sacred: 43 Centuries of Spiritual Poetry by Women* (New York: HarperCollins, 1994).

Marge Piercy, ed., *Early Ripening: American Women's Poetry Now* (New York and London: Pandora, 1987).

Carolyn Forché, ed., *Against Forgetting, Twentieth-Century Poetry of Witness* (New York: W. W. Norton, 1993). This collection includes more than 140 poets from five continents, bearing witness to war, torture, exile, or repression, from the Armenian genocide to Tiananmen Square. Forché, whose own poems often deal with political history, has written an introduction and a brief sketch about each event. Poets writing on the Holocaust include Nelly Sachs, Primo Levi, Paul Celan, Dan Pagis, Irena Klepfisz, and Miklos Radnoti.

Kent Johnson and Craig Paulenich, eds., with an introduction by Gary Snyder, *Beneath a Single Moon, Buddhism in Contemporary American Poetry* (Boston: Shambala, 1991).

Sascha Feinstein and Yusef Komunyakaa, eds., *The Jazz Poetry Anthology* (Bloomington: Indiana University Press, 1991).

Michael Klein, ed., *Poets for Life: Seventy-six Poets Respond to AIDS* (New York: Crown, 1989).

Jason Shinder, ed., *More Light, Father & Daughter Poems, A Twentieth-Century American Selection* (New York: Harcourt Brace, 1993).

Michael Blumenthal, ed., *To Woo & To Wed: Contemporary Poets on Love & Marriage* (New York: Poseidon Press, 1992).

Kathryn and Ross Petras, eds., *Very Bad Poetry* (New York: Random House, 1997). I find some of these hilariously bad, but students are capable of taking them quite seriously and praising rhymes, images, etc. However, certain kindred spirits will laugh with you at James Mcintyre's *Ode on the Mammoth Cheese*—the same ones who find Emmeline Grangerford's bad poems in *The Adventures of Huckleberry Finn* amusing.

Robert Bly, James Hillman, and Michael Meade, eds., *The Rag and Bone Shop of the Heart: Poems for Men* (New York: HarperCollins, 1992). This collection is divided into categories such as wildness, fathers' prayers for sons and daughters (which includes Li-Young Lee, Yeats, Etheridge Knight, Kinnell, Snyder, Rilke, and Stafford), war, language, loving the community and work, anger, zaniness, the cultivated heart. It includes women poets writing about men—Anna Akhmatova, Sharon Olds, Carolyn Kizer, Emily Dickinson—and it draws from various countries and centuries, though the focus is twentieth-century.

Christopher Merrill, ed., *The Forgotten Language: Contemporary Poets and Nature* (Salt Lake City: Gibbs Smith, 1991). An appealing collection that includes plants, insects, animals, and weather.

Alberta Turner, ed., *Fifty Contemporary Poets: The Creative Process* (New York: David McKay, 1977). A fascinating book in which fifty poets pick "one of their own poems they feel is representative of their best current work" and answer Turner's six questions about how they wrote it. Turner is herself a poet, and asks good questions.

Kurt Brown, ed., preface by Edward Hirsch, *Drive, They Said: Poems about Americans and Their Cars* (Minneapolis: Milkweed Editions, 1994). Yes, there is a category "Women in Cars," and those poems are all by women.

5. See note 1, chap. 1. See also the book that was published at the time of the second video series, *The Language of Life—A Festival of Poets,* ed. Jim Haba (New York: Doubleday, 1995). This includes photographs of thirty-four contemporary American poets, including those featured in the video, with at least one poem by each. The poets are interviewed by Bill Moyers.

6. Timpane, 17 (see note 3, chap. 4).

7. Marilyn Hacker, *Selected Poems 1965–1990* (New York: W. W. Norton, 1994) 176–177.

8. Rainer Maria Rilke, *Letters to a Young Poet*, trans. Stephen Mitchell (New York: Random House, Vintage, 1986) 22–23. This is a nice little paperback, almost pocket-size, definitely purse-size. I find my eleventh-graders are ready for some of the ideas in these letters, and those who take their writing seriously sometimes go out and buy their own copies after reading excerpts. Rilke deals with some of the big questions that students this age are asking themselves: Will my parents ever come to understand me? What is love? Are there any answers? Rilke was, after all, writing to a nineteen-year-old.

9. Jane Cooper, *Green Notebook, Winter Road* (Gardiner, ME: Tilbury House, 1993). Cooper writes about the developing self in ways that reflective students can relate to.

10. Gregory Corso, *The Happy Birthday of Death* (New York: New Directions, 1960). Corso's poem "Marriage" is particularly funny in its explorations of the pros and cons from a young man's point of view. It's a great poem to read aloud and discuss—but read it over beforehand!

11. Lawrence Ferlinghetti, *A Coney Island of the Mind* (New York: New Directions, 1958). Students who like Ginsberg and Kerouac generally like Ferlinghetti also.

12. Diane Wakoski, *The Motorcycle Betrayal Poems* (New York: Simon and Schuster, 1971). Many of these poems explore ways a young woman can seek her identity apart from relationships with men. Many girls resonate to Wakoski's rebelliousness and the directness with which she writes about romance and family.

13. Gary Snyder, *No Nature: New and Selected Poems* (New York: Pantheon, 1993). Also see and hear Snyder on video, program # 5, "Here in the Mind," in *The Language of Life* series. Students interested in the outdoors and the environment, or in Buddhism, tend to like this video, and it's interesting to pair it with excerpts from program # 2, "Love's Confusing Joy," in which Coleman Barks reads the 13th century Sufi mystic, Jelaluddin Rumi.

14. Russell Edson, "The Tunnel," in *Selected Poems* (Oberlin, OH: Oberlin College Press, 1994). Edson defies categorization, but he appeals to students with an absurdist or surreal sense of humor, who enjoy surprise. Many of his poems are dialogues between animals or between husband and wife, somewhat reminiscent of the plays of Ionesco or Beckett. They've been labeled prose poems and have been compared to the boxed collages of Joseph Cornell.

15. Anne Sexton, *The Complete Poems* (Boston: Houghton Mifflin, 1981). Sexton's directness in exploring what Freud called "the family romance" and her own sexuality and femaleness, and the way she draws on pop culture as well as the traditions of fairy tale for her bold, striking images, continue to speak to adolescent girls.

16. Maxine Kumin, *Our Ground Time Here Will Be Brief: New and Selected Poems* (New York: Penguin, 1982). My students particularly like her poems about her farm, her animals, her family. Kumin's matter-of-fact way of connecting the deaths of animals and of humans with the regeneration of the earth, the continuity of life, can be helpful for them.

17. Marge Piercy, *Circles on the Water: Selected Poems* (New York: Knopf, 1982). Some girls are uncomfortable with Piercy's very outright, feminist voice, but others feel an affinity right away.

18. Theodore Roethke (see note 3, chap. 2).

19. Linda McCarriston, *Eva-Mary* (Evanston, IL: Triquarterly Books/Northwestern Press, 1991). See also program # 3, "The Field of Time," in *The Language of Life* videos. These poems can be especially powerful for students who have experienced, or who know a friend who has experienced, family violence. McCarriston says, "I had to speak back to the culture that I saw creating and sustaining the ideas that led to this violent situation in the first place."

20. Jane Kenyon, *Otherwise: New and Selected Poems* (St. Paul, MN: Graywolf Press, 1996). I've found Kenyon's poems to be favorites with many girls who are attached to the outdoors, to home, to the details of everyday life, but the poem "Having It Out with Melancholy," while it draws images from these sources, as most of Kenyon's poems do, is a particularly important poem for students who are suffering from clinical depression or have friends in that situation. It also helps teachers understand these students better.

Chapter 12

Talking about a Poem

> ROOMS FULL OF STUDENTS WHO WANT TO TALK AND TALK AND TALK AND
> SPILL OUT IDEAS, TO SUGGEST THINGS TO ME I NEVER THOUGHT OF. IT IS
> LIKE THE HEAPING UP OF ALL THE CHILDREN'S HANDS, ALL THE FAMILY'S
> HANDS, ON THE PARENTAL KNEE IN THE GAME WE USED TO PLAY BY THE
> FIRESIDE.
>
> ROBERT FROST, INTERVIEW WITH JANET MABIE

*W*hen—and where, and how—do we find ourselves talking about poems? If I run into a colleague early Monday morning, while we're getting coffee, and he says he read a terrific Novel over the weekend, I say great, what's it about? And he says, There's this woman—she's very spiritual and she's also very promiscuous, and it's all told from the monkey's point of view in sign language because the woman's third husband is the real audience and he's deaf. And I ask, Is it her monkey, and he says, Well it's hard to tell because she doesn't believe in owning things, that's why she's so pro-miscuous . . .

And we're off. It's easy. But if he asks me about *my* weekend, and I say, It was great, I read this really amazing Poem, he changes the subject. I've tried to talk poetry at the lunch table, too. It puts an immediate damper on the conversation. The closest I've come to success is with the poems I pin up in the faculty bathroom every week. Once Tom said, "You know that poem you put up this week? I don't like it." "Oh?" I said. "No, I don't think it works." "Oh, that's interesting. How come?" "I'd have to think about it." The best day was when the music teacher said, "I took that poem about the pig you put up in the bathroom. I really like it." "Oh, great!" I said. "What did you like about it?" "I like animals," he said.

Occasionally a colleague will ask me what I thought of "that poem in the last *New Yorker*, you know the one—real short, didn't make any sense, I don't know why they print that stuff." There were three short poems that issue. One made sense to me, one didn't but I loved it anyway, and one seemed like it was a translation from some very ancient manuscript that had mostly burned up when the Alexandria Library caught on fire.

Apparently it's not natural to talk about poetry. If you actually wave a poem under someone's nose, shouting "You gotta read this!" they back away because they see in you the gimlet eye of their old English teacher, waiting for them to find the two metaphors and explain line 12. My brothers wouldn't dream of asking to read even the shortest of my poems, though one reads Faulkner and *Moby Dick* for fun and another gets his kicks from *Grove's Dictionary of Music*—all twenty volumes.

My husband has laid down an unspoken law: we read and discuss poetry—mine, John Ashbery's, whoever's—Saturday mornings from 9 till 10:30 during our weekly breakfast at the Rosemont Cafe. How do we talk about poetry? With Ashbery's it's mostly "Just listen to this!" "Wow, isn't that gorgeous (or witty, original, depressing). Where do you think the anteced-ent went to? I mean, are these lines about the same 'you' he mentioned ten lines ago, or are they a whole new deal, maybe it's the dog." With my own poems it's "The middle seems kind of boring. I like the first line. Don't you think 'eagle eyed' is a bit of a cliché?" "But I *meant* it to be a cliché—it's ironic. Look at the context." "I don't see what's so ironic." And, ten minutes later, "Yeah, I see. It works." "No, it doesn't, because I had to explain what was ironic." "Yeah, but now that I *see* it, I like it."

With all the book groups proliferating these days, I know of no poetry-reading group. Groups for *writing* poetry are everywhere; wherever two are gathered together . . . And performances of poetry can be found in every cafe and bookstore, though when I go, I rarely find myself talking with people about the poems we've heard.

I'm happiest when I can read a good poem aloud to a kindred spirit, who I'm pretty sure will catch fire. But I'll know from the look on his face and the tone of voice in which he says "Yes." I don't *need* a lot of talk. "Shop talk" with poet friends is also satisfying: "Did you see the new David Wagoner poem in *Poetry Magazine?*" "Yes, it really moved me—the quietness of the music, it feels very reconciling. I want to show it to my Dad. It's the way I feel about being alone in the woods by the water."

So how should we talk about poetry with students? I think we want to make them confident and comfortable enough with it to offer opinions, recommend specific poets, read aloud favorite passages to friends, pin poems up on their refrigerators, and, ideally, become one of those sensitive, open-minded readers to whom you can take a poem you love, pass it over or read it aloud, and hear a *"Yes."* Or, equally good, an "I love the sounds but I don't get those last couple of lines. What do they say to you?"

In order to help students reach this point we need to make a few resolves. One is, be sensitive to the mood of the class: if, after five minutes talking about a poem, we're getting no response—except from that one dutiful student who will indulge your every conversational whim— we can put that poem aside. There's no absolute necessity to "do" it, even if it *is* Keats's most achingly beautiful sonnet.[1] Try it on another day, maybe grouped with a contemporary poem on a similar subject or in a similar tone.

Or if, on first reading, a poem seems perfectly clear and enjoyable to everyone, we don't have to grind away at it for another twenty minutes. Yes, it contains several examples of synecdoche, but why ruin a good experience, when someone has just commented, "That's real jazzy. It reminds me of the Quincy Troupe poems we read last week, only more like blues. Could we try to write a blues poem?" Count your blessings, grab some Langston Hughes and get the kid in the back row who you just found out plays jazz guitar to read Hughes aloud. And assign a blues instead of the essay you were planning on. Then there's a short story—you're building a blues file now, aren't you—by James Baldwin, some of the most poetic writing about playing jazz that I've ever come across, "Sonny's Blues." It's hard going, but you could read aloud from the last couple pages, where the best images are.

If we've set the right tone in class talk about *student* poems—(1) attentiveness (of body and soul) to the initial reading, (2) praise first, as specific as possible, and (3) questions and suggestions, also specific—we should be able to maintain the same tone in discussions of a Shakespeare sonnet or a Roethke lyric. Since these are apt to be more complex than student poems, we'll just have to reassure students more regularly that "No question is dumb. It's dumb not to ask about what you don't know."

Then there is the issue of "meaning." Adults seem fixated on the idea that every poem has a meaning, every line has a meaning; apparently the teacher invariably asked them to explain what that meaning was—and they always got it wrong. Not till I started writing my own poems did I realize how reductive a paraphrase of a poem or a one-sentence statement of its theme could be. As if you could just siphon off the Meaning, and then sweep the dead poem out the door. Now I see a good poem as a pulsating heart, continually giving off energy, waves of meaning.

So another useful resolve: Don't ask what a poem means. However, it's good to create opportunities to clarify the *facts* in the poem—especially if students reveal confusion. They may not know *why* they're confused. So if a bunch of malcontents sulk into class muttering that last night's poem was really dumb, express sympathy but check them out on *situation, speaker,* and *tone.* Oh, and possible *words* they didn't know they didn't know. And did they notice the *title?* I'm not being sarcastic here; I'm just counting up the number of times when my husband has ignored my carefully chosen title, thus getting off entirely on the wrong foot.

If the poem is "old" or highly allusive or moves in a fashion the class isn't used to, we can give them a break by not assigning it as homework, at least not until it's been given several readings aloud in class and we've offered them some help with the pitfalls. That may not mean explaining allusions, since allusions won't interest them much until they've gotten into the poem and *want* clarification. It may mean something more time-consuming—creating a familiar context in which to talk about the poem.

Suppose you want students to read Keats's sonnet "When I have fears." Let's assume they haven't yet encountered a sonnet. And also, while they may have heard such words as *teeming, garner, glean,* and *relish* (the verb), they may not "know" them in the sense of forming a mental picture when they see them on a page. *Charact'ry* is almost certain to present problems. But none of this is insuperable if they decide they *want* to "get" this poem.

"When I have fears that I may cease to be": A guy in his early twenties wrote this line. About the age you'll be when you finish college. Why might someone that young think he'll not live much longer? What do you imagine yourself doing and feeling when you get through college? Think a bit. . . . Close your eyes and picture yourself. . . . Now try making a list of things you'd be looking forward to, things that would matter to you, maybe even some people you'd like to emulate or live up to. Would the list be much different from a list you'd make right now, at sixteen? Think about it . . . .

Now, imagine not getting to see those things happen, having your experience cut off. Imagine knowing that this is very likely how it's going to be—and you've already seen your older brother's life cut off this way. Close your eyes, tighten yourself up; imagine living with that kind of tension, but imagine it as emotion, not mainly this physical tightness . . .

You have no one you can confide in fully; no one to admit all your feelings to and get comfort. But you can write. In your notebook right now, do a free-write on some of your feelings—fears, desires, specific possibilities you'd be afraid of missing out on—and find some *images*, as you write, to capture the fears and desires.

This is one way to pave the way for Keats. It can lead to a discussion before the class even reads the poem, and you can follow it up by reading aloud, or asking several students to give readings:

When I Have Fears

> When I have fears that I may cease to be
> 　　Before my pen has gleaned my teeming brain,
> Before high-pilèd books in charact'ry,
> 　　Hold like rich garners the full-ripened grain;
> When I behold, upon the night's starred face,
> 　　Huge cloudy symbols of a high romance,
> And think that I may never live to trace
> 　　Their shadows, with the magic hand of chance;
> And when I feel, fair creature of an hour,
> 　　That I shall never look upon thee more,
> Never have relish in the faery power

> Of unreflecting love!—then on the shore
> Of the wide world I stand alone, and think
> Till Love and Fame to nothingness do sink.

Then you can fill them in a little more on Keats's situation—the threat of tuberculosis, his brother Tom's death from it, his own love for Fanny Brawne, maybe a passage from the *Letters* that shows the importance of poetry in his life and his desire to emulate the great poets he admired.

If you want to have the class figure out from looking at this poem the characteristics of a Shakespearian sonnet, you can then get into a discussion, perhaps connected to issues of form that have come up in their own poems, of the effect of expressing strong, deep passion so *formally*. Are there ways in which the "straitjacket" of a sonnet could be inspiring? Comforting? Challenging? Show them a Shakespearian sonnet from the Renaissance and help them see how much more fluid Keats's version is—and how that fluidity focuses us on the big break in the middle of line 12, where all the uncompleted "when" clauses are gathered up as he stands alone "on the shore of the wide world" to think.

It's fine to make use of our expert knowledge of literary history and biography, of language and form. It would be crazy not to. But I think first we have to help students "take charge" of the poem, make it their own. Otherwise they'll grow up to be adults who run away screaming when a friend or lover thrusts a poem at them. "Relevance" isn't a bad word. I know that Emily Dickinson's poems became more relevant to me after my mother's death. We simply have to broaden our students' vision of what is relevant.

There are many poems that can be given much more casual treatment than Keats's sonnet. We ourselves can flip through a book or magazine, reading a poem here, a poem there, enjoying our little flash of reaction, perhaps showing the page to a friend. I like to put packets of poems together, hand them out to a class of, say, freshmen, and ask them to (1) browse at home for twenty minutes, reading silently *and aloud*; (2) choose one poem that particularly catches their interest: practice it by reading it to someone at home; and (3) free-write in response to it for, maybe, twenty minutes in their poetry journal. Next day, these rehearsals and free-writes become the core of our discussion.

Often four or more students will choose the same poem; we hear a couple of readings, discuss the differences—with the people who chose that poem taking the lead—and then let the four talk to us a bit about why they chose it. This may lead anywhere. Suppose "My Father's Love Letters" was on the docket—a poem by Yusef Komunyakaa[2] (recent winner of a Pulitzer Prize):

On Fridays he'd open a can of Jax
After coming home from the mill,
& ask me to write a letter to my mother
Who sent postcards of desert flowers
Taller than men. He would beg,
Promising to never beat her
Again. Somehow I was happy
She had gone, & sometimes wanted
To slip in a reminder, how Mary Lou
Williams' "Polka Dots & Moonbeams"
Never made the swelling go down.
His carpenter's apron always bulged
With old nails, a claw hammer
Looped at his side & extension cords
Coiled around his feet.
Words rolled from under the pressure
Of my ballpoint: Love,
Baby, Honey, Please.
We sat in the quiet brutality
Of voltage meters & pipe threaders,
Lost between sentences . . .
The gleam of a five-pound wedge
On the concrete floor
Pulled a sunset
Through the doorway of his toolshed.
I wondered if she laughed
& held them over a gas burner.
My father could only sign
His name, but he'd look at blueprints

& say how many bricks
Formed each wall. This man,
Who stole roses & hyacinth
For his yard, would stand there
With eyes closed & fists balled,
Laboring over a simple word, almost
Redeemed by what he tried to say.

The student who read it aloud for us leads off. (All comments below are by individual students—nine or ten—except for the comments labeled "Me"):

"I liked this one a lot—I guess 'cause I have a friend whose dad used to beat on her mom. Now they're divorced and he's married again, and I kind of wonder if he's that mean to this other wife."

"Did he beat up your friend, too?"

"No, at least if he did she didn't tell me. But I don't think so. She never showed me any marks."

"God, that's so unreal. Why would somebody stay with a guy like that?"

"Wouldn't you be scared what he could do to you if he left you?"

ME: "What did the wife in the poem do?"

"She left. And the kid's glad she did."

"But he must miss her. It's funny he doesn't say that."

"Yeah, but he's mainly afraid she might come back and get hurt some more. He wants to remind her somethingorother never made the swelling go down. What's 'Mary Lou Williams?'"

"She's probably a singer, 'cause Polka Dots & Moonbeams sounds like a song."

"Oh, that didn't make any sense to me at all."

ME: "But you liked the poem anyway? That didn't bother you, not knowing what that line meant?"

"No, I just figured it was something both parents knew about."

"But it makes it better if you guess, 'cause he must have played that music to try to make up, after he hurts her. Maybe it was their favorite song."

"Oh—I never got that."

ME: "Is it hard to picture your parents having a favorite song—going on dates?"

"Not really. My mom was a flower child. She and my Dad went to Beatles concerts, and they've got all their old records."

"I can't imagine what my parents would have talked about on dates. They never talk now except when they argue about me."

ME: "Do you think the couple in the poem argued?"

"Yeah, sure. That's why he beat her up all the time."

"No, I don't think so. He doesn't talk. He just hits."

"There's a word in the first line I didn't get—Jax. What's Jax?"

"I thought it was something to wash his hands with."

"I think it's the name of a beer—'cause it's Friday, he gets home from work at the mill, and he wants to relax."

"Oh, maybe he drinks a lot and that's why he hits her."

"I don't think so. It's just Fridays. But maybe he drinks a lot on those nights and that's when he loses it."

ME: "Could you four who read this one go to the mural and put up your favorite lines and images? And let's maybe have four more volunteers who *didn't* choose it, go up and add things you liked when Jan read it aloud—take another quick look at it in the packet if you need to. Everybody else, go through the poem on the page, and mark the parts you think are especially strong."

[They do, and then we all crowd around the mural paper and take turns reading the phrases aloud—a kind of distillation of the poem.]

postcards of desert flowers taller than men . . . a claw hammer looped at
his side . . . words rolled from under the pressure of my ballpoint . . .
quiet brutality . . . pulled a sunset through the doorway . . . words rolled
. . . laboring over a simple word . . . eyes closed & fists balled . . . almost
redeemed by what he tried to say . . . quiet brutality . . . quiet brutality

ME: "Great choices! Notice how many are concrete—images. Did you feel the physical difference between the son's words *rolling out* and the father's fists balled and eyes closed, *laboring* to get a word? I'd include more of the details of his carpenter skills—the apron bulging with nails, the extension cords coiled around his feet— looped and coiled—do they add anything to this scene?"

"Yeah, I didn't notice before but it's, like, the two sides of his father—good with his hands but brutal with them, too. All those tools bulge and loop and coil—they're surrounding him, they're, like, who he is."

"They're the picture the son will always have of him—sitting there next to the five-pound wedge."

"Yeah, in the sunset."

ME [thinking ahead to future writing possibilities]: "Close your eyes for a moment and think—What's the picture that comes to your mind of your mother or father, the picture you think you'll always see, if you live to be ninety? . . . Jot that down in your journal right now, just in case you ever want to use it in a poem." [We all write for a minute or two.]

ME: "So the tools work really well as images. What about the flowers. Would the poem lose anything if all the flowers weren't in it?"

"All what flowers?"

"Oh, she means the roses and hyacinth he steals for his yard—well, they're like his soft side, like when he makes the son write Baby, Honey, Love."

"Oh, wow, look, it's the soft side he means when the son—is the son the writer? Anyway, the poem says the father's almost redeemed by what he tried to say. His fists are all balled up and he can't write—

he can't say stuff. But he'd like to be *softer*. He'd like to be more open."

"Yeah, he talks with his hands. [Laughter] No, I mean it. He's the strong, silent type, but that's bad 'cause you have to be able to, like communicate."

"That's such a stereotype. My dad talks to me and my mom a lot.

ME: "Well, let's ask the guys. When you're with your best friend, do you talk a lot? What do you talk about?"

"We don't have to say much. We do stuff together—basketball, guitar. We know each other pretty well."

"Yeah. It's better that way. My sister's on the phone all the time with her girlfriends. It's just gossip. I don't know what they have to talk about."

ME: "Well, sometimes I have a misunderstanding with a friend and I want to talk it out. But I can do this with a few of my male friends, too—not as many, though. What do you two guys do if you get mad or hurt the other's feelings?"

"We joke about it. Or we just leave it alone and go home."

"Yeah, you guys just punch each other around. You're so childish!"

"It's better than crying all the time and getting your feelings hurt. You have to learn to take it and forget it."

ME: "What do you think it would be like if these two really different attitudes had to live together as husband and wife?"

"I guess they'd both have to change a little. Or else get divorced."

ME: "I don't want to press too hard, but I do wonder about those postcards the mother sends with desert flowers—more flowers!— taller than men. Would the poem lose anything if they weren't in there?"

"Where's that? Oh, I didn't see that."

"It's neat because it's a kind of put-down of him. Like she's started a new life, she doesn't need him, she's got the flowers."

ME: "I've never been in the desert. Anybody here?"

"Yeah. We went to New Mexico. And California. They have those
real tall, white flowers—yucca, I think it's called."

ME: "Anybody want to say anything more about this poem?"

Silence. I'd have liked to get into the lines about the son wondering if
the mother laughed when she got the letters, and burned them, and what it
must feel like for the son to imagine this possibility—to miss her but know
her contempt for his dad, and how about his complicated feelings toward
this father? And if he's already good with words, maybe even a poet in the
making, how's that affecting the father/son relationship. And the whole
issue of power. I also wanted to point out some line breaks, since students
had been asking about them in a couple of their own poems. But attention is
starting to wander, and there are other students who want to read their
poems. So we go on.

There are always a lot of variables to think about: the mood in the room,
the number of poems people want to get through, the difficulty of the
poems, whether our emphasis is on writing or reading that week, how long
the class has been together and how much sharing of poems they've done.
This discussion took place in the spring. I distinctly remember my disap-
pointment at the group's *first* attempt to talk about a poem—e. e.
cummings's love poem, "somewhere i have never travelled, gladly beyond."[3]
It lasted all of five minutes and consisted of three students saying that "the
images were real good" but agreeing that the voice was cynical and the girl
was manipulative and this was so obvious that why should we waste any
more time on the poem? I was baffled, because I couldn't get them interested in pinning down exactly which words or lines had given them this
impression. Fortunately, as they became more serious about their own
writing in the following months, the talk got better.

I try not to shut off a line of thought if it feels as though a lot of energy's
invested in it, but I also have to be timekeeper. If important aspects of the
poem don't come up, I'll raise them myself, but even then I try to avoid the
inquisitorial mode. I also try—but often forget—to ask at the beginning of a
class how many people chose which poem, so I can time the discussion
accordingly.

A typical packet I gave to the freshmen this fall to spark discussion included Russell Edson,[4] Mary Oliver,[5] Sharon Olds,[6] Theodore Roethke,[7] e. e. cummings, Charles Simic,[8] and Emily Dickinson[9]—the specific pieces ranging from a sci-fi type of poem about living backwards, to a bird poem, a subway poem about racism, a father/son poem, an animal poem, a surreal poem about how Death spends the day, and a poem about the imagination. Each got chosen by someone, but cummings's love poem and Charles Simic's "death poem" called "Eyes Fastened with Pins" were the favorites.

I've learned over the years that scheduling too many discussions vitiates the effectiveness of this approach. Even the most enthusiastic poets will get tired of talking about poems, whereas if you allow anticipation to build a little and alternate discussion with writing in class, performing, working in small groups, peer-editing, silent reading, you get higher quality talk. In the discussion of Komunyakaa's poem we touched on its relation to "real life" and some issues of craft, clarified an allusion and an unfamiliar word, arrived at a couple of psychological insights, at least raised the issue of whether speaker and poet were one and the same—though we didn't resolve it—and probably made a good shot at discussing "meaning." Though I didn't indicate this, some students participated who had *not* chosen the poem themselves, and this is important. I don't want three-quarters of the class to get the impression that they have no stake in this poem; they need to gain the confidence to leap in, and they need to learn how to attend to whatever poem is "up" rather than tune out till their poem comes around. This is part of building community, and if it works, you get to hear students praising other students' insights: "Oh, wow, I never noticed that." And sometimes the teacher can join in—"Oh, wow, neither did I."

Notes

1. John Keats, "When I have fears . . ." in *Keats, Poetical Works* (London: Oxford University Press, 1967) 366.

2. Yusef Komunyakaa, "My Father's Love Letters" (see note 3, chap. 10).

3. e.e. cummings, "somewhere i have never travelled, gladly beyond," in *Poems 1923–1954* (New York: Harcourt, Brace & World, 1954) 263.

4. Edson, "Antimatter," 125 (see note 14, chap. 11).

5. Mary Oliver, "Harvest Moon—the Mockingbird Sings in the Night" in *Twelve Moons* (Boston: Little, Brown and Co., 1979) 38–39.

6. Sharon Olds, "On the Subway" in *The Gold Cell* (New York: Knopf, 1987) 5–6.

7. Roethke, "My Papa's Waltz" and "The Meadow Mouse," 43 and 219 (see note 3, chap. 2).

8. Charles Simic, "Eyes Fastened with Pins" in *Selected Poems 1963–1983* (New York: George Braziller, 1990) 125.

9. Dickinson, "The brain—is wider than the Sky—" 312–313 (see note 1, chap. 2).

Chapter 13

With Portfolio

THE THEATER OF ANY POEM IS A COLLECTION OF DECISIONS ABOUT SPACE AND TIME—HOW ARE THESE WORDS TO LIE ON THE PAGE, WITH WHAT PAUSES, WHAT HEADLONG MOTION, WHAT PHRASING, HOW CAN THEY MEET THE BREATH OF THE SOMEONE WHO COMES ALONG TO READ THEM?

ADRIENNE RICH, *WHAT IS FOUND THERE*

"So, Cam, why do you want to include this dream poem in your portfolio? I thought you didn't like it?"

"Well, I didn't. But Mike suggested starting it farther down—right here, with the first image—and cutting the dumb ending about how I woke up—and I have an idea for a new ending, so I think I'm going to like it."

"Great! I'm really curious to see the new ending. Would you read the whole thing aloud from where you're going to start it? And

really listen to the line breaks? And see if it might make more sense
on the page in two stanzas?"

It's near the end of the semester, two weeks before freshman poetry portfolios are due, and everyone has signed up for a conference. Some want to run
their final selections by me—"Do you think the tooth poem's got a better
ending than the one about my grandfather?" Some want to know whether
they can get away with certain daring experiments in punctuation. Cam has
suddenly started taking himself seriously as a writer, as he realizes that a
partner will be reading and writing about his portfolio, and he doesn't want
to "look dumb." Forget the fact that I'm putting a grade on the thing that will
count for half his term mark in English.

   Portfolios have been in the air recently, and as I thought about using
them with my students, I realized how much I always gain from having to
go through my poems to make groupings for competitions, applications to
artist colonies and grant committees, etc. On those occasions I'm forced to
survey my work, to revise, to consider patterns I haven't noticed before—
and to assess whether I'm growing as a writer.

   And I have to think about which of my poems have the best chance of
communicating with new readers. Are some of them too private? Too
explanatory, too bullying? Which ones invite the reader in but also leave
space for his imagination to work? What order should they go in? Although
strangers will ultimately pass judgment, I'm being forced to make my own
assessment. As the head of our art department is fond of saying, when he
requires his artists to select work to submit for the school art show, "You
must commit to the work."

   Now, after two years' experience with poetry portfolios, I realize they
have addressed one of my chief weaknesses as a teacher. I always valued
spontaneity and equated it with authenticity. I wanted to steer my students
away from working for grades. I wanted classes to be exciting, a little off-the-
wall, a stream of surprises. But in pursuing these goals, I forgot a couple of
very human needs: to have something specific to strive for, to know by what
standards your striving will be judged, and to know how you can do better—
before it's "too late."

   With the result that students were more worried about grades than ever.
"So if you don't grade our poems, do they count? Do we get credit for revising them?" I didn't want to grade their poems; I wanted them to revise

poems for the love of it. I didn't want to give tests on poetry. I didn't want to grade their poetry notebooks, which were full of exploratory or "free" writing—spontaneous rambling, stream-of-consciousness—as well as aborted first drafts, trial lines, doodles, quotations, news headlines, dreams.

Looking back on this year's freshmen and on my junior/senior poetry class, I'm very happy I decided to try portfolios. All my freshmen wrote in the end-of-year assessments that writing (and in many cases, poetry) had been the area in which they'd improved most—and many chose the portfolio presentations as the year's most memorable classes. My older students, whose one-semester course had been due to culminate in readings from their portfolios, were so eager for this reading that when a blizzard struck, they set up a phone tree and arranged to come in during the day scheduled for make-up exams, which they could have taken as a holiday.

I announced in September that rather than put "final" grades on pieces as I read them, I would set up a rubric, with help from the students: a chart that writers and peer editors and I could all use to assess various stages of a work-in-progress—and that everything they turned in could be considered a draft, capable of being revised with an eye to inclusion in the portfolio at the end of the term. We agreed on the number of pieces to be presented—five poems with various drafts attached, and an introductory essay to guide the reader.

The introduction should itself be a strong piece of writing, and would include reasons why the writer selected each piece, an *ars poetica*—what he had come to believe about poetry, perhaps what specific qualities he admired in particular poems by other poets—and a description of how his own poems tended to take shape. I suggested that each student try to find an image or metaphor to help characterize himself as a writer. The essay should also include an account of how he felt he had grown as a poet during the semester and what he'd still like to accomplish.

Because the images that students found for describing themselves as writers were often so lively and so telling, I wish now that I had required everyone to do this:

> The way I have approached just about everything in my life until
> this set of poems has been a bit like catching frogs. Taking great
> care to search for the perfect plot of not-too-soggy grass to plant my
> foot on its next step into the irreversible future, so that I may gaze
> upon the surface of a wide and deep lake. Perhaps I'm compulsive.

> Certainly I'm a perfectionist. But I think what I realized in writing
> poetry this year is that catching frogs in this manner may work all
> right in other parts of life, but it doesn't work that well with poetry.
> What follows is a collection of the poetry that I am most proud of. It
> is the poetry that I dove head first in a lake to get, and I was sur-
> prised to find what swam up to me. . . . My last poem, *Fear*, I
> consider to be a real triumph. I sat down with my starting line,
> obtained rather randomly: *Fear is a purple crocodile*, and wrote a
> long, rich free-write. . . . I wasn't standing on the edge of a lake
> straining my eyes for a large, moving poem, I was swimming
> through the water inside of my poem, collecting bits of material.

We agreed that a partner would read the portfolio—the poems first,
silently and aloud, then the introduction, then the poems again. She'd write
a two to three-page critique addressed to the author, commenting on specific strengths and weaknesses she saw in the poems and in the revising,
responding to ideas about poetry in the introduction, and indicating ways in
which this essay was or wasn't helpful in orienting her to the poems.

Later, just before portfolios were due, I asked, "How should we pair up?"
Some students said, "Put me with anybody, it's fine," but there were enough
who didn't feel this way so that finally we agreed each person could give me
names of three or four classmates she'd be most comfortable working with
and could name one person she'd rather *not* work with. I would take it from
there. Interestingly, the one person with whom almost no one wanted to
work was the only kid who hadn't taken the peer editing seriously so far.

I let my classes keep their poems in a folder, or fastened into their
poetry notebooks, including the various drafts. At the end of the term, when
everyone selected their pieces for the portfolio, I would ask them to design
their own "packaging"—container, cover title—that would in some way
reflect the nature of the poems or the poet and would prepare us for what
was inside the package.

Of first importance, I felt, was to arrive at some standards for assessing
our work. I didn't want to hand out a prefabricated list; I wanted the student
poets to go through the process of discovery together—to recognize that they
themselves were basically in agreement (I hoped!) on what made a good
poem. One day, after we'd been reading and writing poems for three or four
weeks, I asked the freshmen to talk about what things seemed necessary for

a poem to "work"—to hold their attention, to stay with them. As they talked, I took notes—which put the onus of discussion on them.

"The poem has to be honest about feelings."

"It has to be real."

"No it doesn't. You can make things up. You can imagine."

"Well, I just meant the *feelings* have to be real."

"But if you had a good imagination, you could make people believe you know how some homeless guy feels. Or like that poet who wrote about Death as if he were a person—but he wouldn't really know what Death would be like."

"But when you read that poem, you know Death isn't really a guy with daughters who do his laundry and all that. You know he's just making it up."

"Yeah, it's, like, personification."

"Ooooh."

"Images make all the difference."

"Yeah, like Death not having a dime to make a phone call. And the flowers and tools in that abuse poem."

"Rhyme can keep you from saying what you really want to say. I'm much better off now that I stopped rhyming."

"But rhyme can help you sometimes. I mean—I can't explain this—when I did that rhyming poem last week it made me say some words that I wouldn't ever have thought about using before. I think rhyming and non-rhyming poems can both be good."

"But listen, you know what's bad about rhymes? You know when they're coming. I like surprises."

"I like poems on surprising subjects. Poems can be about anything. Like Quincy Troupe's poem on Magic Johnson."

"Or that guy who wrote about his brother and AIDS."

"Poems need good words. The parts of poems that we write up on the wall usually have good sounds."

"But not big, show-off words. They just have to be right. Like really specific."

"They have to sound good."

"That makes them easier to remember."

"Poems have to make pictures you can really get into."

"The first line needs to pull you in. Sometimes you need to start the poem farther down because the first lines are real lame because you didn't know what you wanted to say yet."

"If you explain too much, it's like an essay."

"Yeah, or a newspaper. But you have to explain *some*."

"Not if you have the right words. You can show stuff and let people figure out what you mean."

"Yeah, but I hate poems I can't figure out. Like some real old poem that doesn't make any sense."

"But if it's too obvious, maybe you won't read it again. I like there to be some mystery that makes me keep thinking about it."

"Poems don't always have to be heavy. They can be kind of funny even about serious stuff. Like the one about Death not having a dime. Or Sam's one about his dog dying—there were some funny parts in it."

"But you can't jump around too much. It's gotta all fit together like a puzzle. Maybe there can be different parts, but they all have to fit."

"You have to think about line breaks. Not run over the line too many times or it doesn't work. And not end lines on dumb, little words."

"Yeah, line breaks can make a rhythm, like in Quincy Troupe. But I guess rhymes make a beat, too, when they come at the end over and over."

"Oh yeah, repetition can be good. It really emphasizes stuff."

"But when you revise, there's usually repetition that doesn't work. It sounds like an accident."

"Adjectives are good."

"If you like *flowery* poems."

"Well, they have to be the right adjectives. And strong verbs are important."

"And poems should have, you know, poetic license. I like poems
that break rules—like no punctuation. And no capital letters."

"You can use slang. Like Quincy Troupe. You can use any words you
want."

"But not clichés."

"Yeah, but it might be a cliché to some reader but not to you."

"The ending has to be good. It shouldn't explain the poem."

"No, and it shouldn't sum it up, like 'I love my dog.'"

From all this I took a shot at putting together a checklist that we could
use in peer editing and that I could fill in during a conference with a student. When I had boiled down their ideas about what a poem should be, it
looked like this:

1. *Tone* (speaker's attitude toward situation)—clear; can be implied;
don't explain too much
2. *Words*—fresh; precise; to convey tone and situation and speaker; to
create memorable images and sounds
3. *Structure*—to fit tone and situation; nothing extra; an inviting first
line; a strong ending that doesn't explain or sum up; that leaves us
thinking and feeling
4. *Overall*—poem should reflect poet's commitment to the material
and the reader

I tried to keep technical language to a minimum, so that freshmen could
actually use this checklist themselves. I also put together my own one-page
handout called "Some Pointers on Revising," which went into greater detail
and included suggestions such as "Put checks next to any word or phrase
you love for its sound and/or the picture it makes. Do you have a lot of
checks?" And "Mark for prosiness—too much explaining; make us *see* how
scary, don't tell us you were scared." And "Circle all the clutter—little words
like *the, a, an, in, out, sort of, very, really,* etc. See whether your poem can do
without some of these." And "Does the poem move somewhere by the end?
Does it need to go further? Try starting a new draft, using the last line as
your first."

At first, students' willingness and ability to revise their poems varied wildly. Some students, including some of the seniors, seemed able to revise only when sitting next to my desk in conference; given an assignment to go home, choose a poem, apply the checklists, and create a new draft, they returned with one word cut, or one line changed. "I like it the way it is."

I sympathized. I remember sessions with a mentor, a gifted, successful poet with three books out, in which I raised objections to every question she asked; I loved my poem the way it was. Finally she sent me on my way with the dictum that I seemed to have reached a plateau and just wasn't ready to go any further. Of course, there is always, in theory, the possibility that a poem is finished; the first draft is "perfect." But more likely the author is either too emotionally involved with it to re-envision it or isn't getting any more energy from it—has just lost interest. One advantage of the portfolio is that in selecting a poem for it, you are committing yourself to making it the best poem you can; pieces you dislike, that never went beyond exercises, you can abandon.

With my older students I occasionally created a workshop situation, in which whoever was reading her poem aloud had to sit in silence afterwards while classmates described what they'd heard, what they were confused about, what felt like the strongest parts.

But of course, other people's interpretations of your poem can feel totally pigheaded. A poet friend once said, "Don't leave any holes in your poem for the reader to fall through, because he'll find them and then turn it into his poem, the one he wanted you to write." On the other hand, you want your poem to invite others to engage with it; you want to leave enough space in the weave.

For most students, practice helps. After one conference and one peer-editing session, Melissa, a freshman, came to me with a new poem she'd started in class the day we drew and free-associated on an object—in her case, an apple. "I really like a lot of the words in this, and I know I want to use it in the portfolio, but it needs some work." She'd already diagnosed a problem—the structure. It was just a jumbled mass of details. She decided she wanted to move from the outside of the apple into the heart. She wanted to start with someone taking a bite, and trace the sensations from the skin into the core. She was taking much more responsibility for this conference than for the previous one. "If I move this section up here, that makes the direction of the bite clearer, doesn't it?" She knew where she wanted help from me: "I want to describe the shape of the apple when a bite's been taken out of it. See, this is how I want you to see it"—and she drew a little sketch. "But I need a word for the shape you make that goes in instead of sticking out." "Concave?" I asked. "Yeah, thanks." And she wrote it down.

Many of the students needed to raise their sights in terms of language. This meant cutting out clutter as much as it did finding fresher, more precise words. They needed to chip away at the marble so the shape could emerge—but for some it was hard to envision a shape. To recognize what the poem had to offer. One boy, a trained singer who had attended a boys choir school that concertized in Europe, wrote a long poem about a specific Christmas concert in Germany when he felt homesick for his family. "What's the most important part of the poem for you?" I asked, and he pointed to the last fifteen lines—exactly the part I liked best. "Can you imagine cutting out most of the preceding lines? If you did, what information would you need to fit into the last fifteen lines somewhere?"

I was impressed that Matt could entertain this suggestion with equanimity; one hates to "waste" so much writing. But the long-winded account of training for the concert and flying to Europe and how the boys arranged themselves on the stage was really rather drab prose, cut up into lines of free verse. The last fifteen lines were much more evocative, capturing the way Matt's thoughts of a family Christmas wove into the singing; they just needed a few details to clarify the situation.

My Song

> there we stood
> in our bold uniforms
> we sang the second encore
> my song
>
> we were halfway
> through the piece by Rutter
> the Lord lift up the light
> of his countenance upon you
> I began to think of my family
> at home

at dinner
one chair needs to be filled
and give you peace
how I need to call them
when we get to our host families
and give you peace
tears swelled in my eyes
never did I long for them so much
Amen

A number of students were afflicted with an excess of adjectives; if one adjective was good, two must be better. I pointed out the dull rhythms and the heaviness that recurring pairs of adjectives can produce: "gentle and soft," "dreary and desolate," "fresh and new," "cold and wintry." We discussed which one of the pair was the better, in terms of sound, picture, feeling. Or maybe they simply needed a more exact *noun*, and both adjectives could go. I quoted something Sharon Olds had said at a poetry workshop: "When I revise, the first things I cut are adjectives and self-pity."

Flabby verb phrases were also popular; I pushed for one-word active verbs—not "he had a desire to" but "he desired." Some students insisted on a plethora of present participles, especially to start off a poem. "I guess I like them because they make the poem flow," one girl admitted. At the start of the year, "flowing" seemed to be the supreme accolade. "I love your poem, it really flows." To start a poem with a direct statement seemed too mundane, too prosaic, when you could start with "Sparkling in the sun, sinking, whirling, spinning in a dance. Dreaming. Wishing I were on a white beach, dabbling my toes in the waves, wondering if he liked me, remembering . . . ."

The portfolio project increased student interest in line breaks, stanza breaks, and punctuation. They began to notice a poem's look on the page and the way this look dictated how the poem would sound. e. e. cummings had been the first to stir their interest in all these things with his graphic poem on loneliness, which he arranges on the page so that we contemplate "one leaf" at the same time as we're reading "loneliness."[1] And William Carlos Williams's poems about the old woman eating plums, the cat climbing over the jam closet, and the red wheel barrow all led students to ask "How come? Why are the line breaks so weird?"[2]

I like to give students a Shakespeare sonnet written out in a prose paragraph and Williams's cat and jam closet poem written out the same way. "Read each of these over a few times and then try lining them out so they look more like poetry, in whatever form you think best suits them. Most students, given enough time, can spot the rhyme pattern of the sonnet and realize this dictates where each line must end; they have much more trouble figuring it out from the *meter*—even after having read a Shakespeare play—so I suggest they count the syllables of the first two rhyming lines and see if that helps them hear the pattern of beats. I throw conversational lines at them in iambic pentameter—I went to town to buy a pound of fish; I took it home and put it in a dish; etc., etc. Sometimes this helps.

Take a look at the poem by Williams written out as prose. Consider the subject—the cat climbing very delicately over the closet so as not to break those flowerpots—and then try suiting the sound to the sense, arranging the actions into individual lines and stanzas:

POEM

As the cat climbed over the top of the jamcloset first the right forefoot carefully then the hind stepped down into the pit of the empty flowerpot

A few good rules of thumb for line breaks, I tell the freshmen, are as follows: Don't *enjamb* too often (that is, don't carry over the sentence to the next line without punctuation), or you'll lose the irregularity you wanted and just create another kind of pattern. You can use enjambment to achieve a very jagged effect, perhaps to disturb or disorient us or simply to emphasize a particular word or create suspense. In general, in free verse you can let breathing be a guide to breaking the line. Also, in general, it's best to end a line on a strong word. Take Whitman, whose long, bounding lines are such a contrast to Williams's: his lines end more often than not on a concrete word. Here, on a sample page from "Song of Myself" are his end words: *rest, limbs, brush, dark, floor, meadow, hides, rafters, cylinders, ribs, down, sand, smoke, water, currents.*

Punctuation—or its absence—is simply a matter of consistency. Not that students found this simple: "But I want it to *flow*—I don't want a period there. e. e. cummings doesn't use periods *or* capital letters." Why had I taught them about "poetic license" if only to snatch it away?

"Look at cummings's "Buffalo Bill."[3] How many sentences in it? Two?
Okay. The second one starts with "Jesus," so that's capitalized because it's a
proper noun, not necessarily as the start of a new sentence—but we know
it's a new thought because it's on a new *line* all by itself; we don't need a
period. Same with the next clause, which is also a new idea—a real turn in
the poem. That, too, is on a new line. And wherever we'd expect a comma
we have a line break or indentation, except for the rush of claypigeons:
'onetwothreefourfive'—bang, bang, bang, bang, bang, no pause between the
bullets: he broke them "just like that." The spaces and indentations do the
work of punctuation, and he's *consistent*—no punctuation at all, and no caps
except for proper names. So decide on one approach to these two matters,
whatever will best guide your reader to the way you want the poem to
sound and mean. And stick with it."

    Buffalo Bill's
    defunct
            who used to
              ride a watersmooth-silver
                      stallion
    and break onetwothreefourfive pigeonsjustlikethat
                                      Jesus
    he was a handsome man
                    and what i want to know is
    how do you like your blueeyed boy
    Mister Death

Revising poems for the portfolio can also prompt an interest in stanzaic
form. I make a point of including in the freshman packets some poems
written in couplets or tercets or quatrains, as well as a villanelle and a
sestina. While very few of my students choose to write in these forms, they
do begin to see reasons for dividing their own free verse into "stanzas" or
verse paragraphs. "I could show where my poem changes from a memory to
right now if I split it into two stanzas," Mike said. "Maybe when my apple
poem moves from outside to inside, I should leave a space," Melissa suggested. They begin to see *how form can express meaning*. When we write
memory poems, we experiment with Gary Snyder's meditative rhythm,

leaving some spaces between two words on the same line—time for
memory, for associations, for breathing and musing. [4]

> *I don't mind   living this way*
> *Green hills   the long blue beach*
> *But sometimes   sleeping in the open*
> *I think back   when I had you.*
>   ("Four Poems for Robin")

Stanzas that are determined by rhyme and meter, especially intricate
interlocking rhymes like the pattern in terza rima—even contemporary
variations that use slant rhyme or irregular rhymes—can be very intimidat-
ing to student poets. To my seniors' rebellious souls the "rules" of a
villanelle are annoyingly dogmatic—like the Dress Code. Who needs them?
The music and mystery of Roethke's "The Waking" [5] and the power of Dylan
Thomas's "Do Not Go Gentle into That Good Night," [6] two great villanelles,
generally win them over—as readers; the irony in Elizabeth Bishop's beautiful "One Art"—"The art of losing isn't hard to master"—often eludes them. [7]
But few students are inspired to try writing a villanelle or sestina, except as
a challenging puzzle.

So I talk about how certain emotions and situations can call forth certain
traditional forms, maybe because the poet identifies with the voice of an
earlier master of that form. The villanelle lends itself to expressing mystery, or
obsession. And I explain how poets have sometimes found that in dealing with
very painful or frightening situations—rape, for example, or the loss of a par-
ent, or intense depression, or abuse—the discipline of form enables them to
objectify or transcend their emotions through the process of shaping the poem.

Students assume that a poet always chooses a form in advance and
applies it to the material like a cookie cutter. This can feel very artificial to
them. So I explain, "Some poets do start out knowing what form they want
to use, but many wait to see what the poem seems to dictate as they write it.
Here's a recent poem of mine that I thought would be all one free verse
paragraph until I began to hear some traces of rhyme—*pond, dawn, stone,
moon*—at the ends of lines.

Then, a little later, when I still knew there was more to say, I noticed I
had what felt like two sections, of seven lines each; seven is a magical, fairy

tale number, and I liked its imbalance for this particular poem, that was being so elusive and seemed to be trying to breach a mysterious barrier between life and death. So I tried to discover in seven more lines whatever meaning the poem's central image had to offer me. It was a poem about the moonstone ring my mother had left me, which I'd already written about once, four months earlier."

Again, Moonstone

> *Your ring is a mountain pond*
> *in thick, gray dawn*
> *where I can't see your face*
> *or even mine. Water weighs*
> *more than we think*
> *gathered in tear or stone.*
> *I was always drawn by the moon*
>
> *but yours is too heavy for wear.*
> *It sits by me in my purse,*
> *dense, secret. Last night*
> *I wore it to a concert*
> *where it drenched the songs*
> *in fishlight, silver shaken from a past*
> *that felt like drowning.*
>
> *And I think, If I scale myself,*
> *cut right on through,*
> *might the ring be there,*
> *swallowed whole, heavy and smooth*
> *from so much wear I'd know*
> *I hold you hard, as music,*
> *once felt, is hard to lose.*

I always hope that in preparing their portfolios, students will find themselves thinking about how art is made—even if they don't have the sophistication to articulate these thoughts very clearly. I tell them a little about my own revising process—how some of my poems have been sitting in a notebook for seven years but still have the power to engage my imagination. I quote the contemporary poet Li-Young Lee, who told students that a poem can go on giving back energy that the poet can use in revising it—until he realizes it's finished or it has nothing left to offer him.

I show them the crossed-out drafts in my notebook that led, finally, to a poem printed on the page of a magazine. Though I hasten to add that no amount of revising guarantees that a poem will get published!

Not every student has the patience to take a poem through more than, say, two or three drafts. And sometimes a second draft is not an improvement—even the reverse! A strong line may get cut, perhaps because a student editor criticized it, or because the writer was worried that it was "flowery" or "didn't flow." I remind the class to keep reading their work aloud, over and over, and to get other people to read it back to them so they can hear it more objectively. Sometimes a student will say, "But you're not reading it right! Here, let me show you." This is a good opportunity to look hard at the arrangement of lines on the page—breaks, punctuation, etc. How do they lead us to read the poem?

Finally the day comes. We're all excited. The freshmen have made their selections from all the poems they've written during the term—"wrong dream" poems, body poems, poems written to music, object poems, memory poems, blues, poems in response to Quincy Troupe, poems beginning with a stolen line, poems treating an emotion metaphorically, snapshot poems, poems about poetry. The ritual passing of portfolio from writer to partner takes place, with much oohing at cover designs and titles.

We spend the rest of the class in silent reading, with partners taking time out to inscribe lines and phrases they especially like up on the poetry mural. The period ends with a group reading of these lines. Poets go home and read their partners' responses and have one final shot at revising. Then, three days later, I get to read the Selected Works, including introductions and partners' letters.

Before I produce grades and comments, we have a Poetry Café—with a spotlight for the readers (everyone chooses at least one poem to read from the portfolio), candles on red-and-white checked tablecloths, bagels and cream cheese, and much applause.

Hearing these final drafts read aloud by their authors helps me in assessing—not only the portfolios and the students' growth as poets and critics, but the power of poetry to build a community of writers.

Notes

1. e. e. cummings, "le(a)f" in *Another E. E. Cummings*, sel. Richard Kostelanetz (New York: Liveright, 1998) 137.

2. Williams, "To a Poor Old Woman," vol. 1, 383 (see chap. 3, note 3); "Poem," vol. 1, 352; "The Red Wheelbarrow," vol. 1, 224.

3. e. e. cummings, "Buffalo Bill's" in *Poems*, 50 (see note 3, chap. 12).

4. Snyder, "Siwashing it out once in Siuslaw Forest" from "Four Poems for Robin," in *The Back Country* (New York: New Directions, 1968).

5. Roethke (see note 3, chap. 2).

6. Dylan Thomas, "Do Not Go Gentle into That Good Night," 128 (see note 2, chap. 10).

7. Elizabeth Bishop, "One Art" in *Geography III* (New York: Farrar, Straus & Giroux, 1976), 40.

Chapter 14

Expanding the Circle

MANY OF OUR POEMS . . . OFFER THE TRUTHS OF OUTRAGE AND THE TRUTHS OF POSSIBILITY.

MURIEL RUKEYSER, *THE LIFE OF POETRY*

*P*oetry can transform a classroom into a community. A sixteen-year-old finding words and images with which to explore her feelings about a painful love affair can become more responsive to a teacher's loss of her mother, or to a minority student suffering the pain of racial discrimination. The teacher writing about her mother's death may already be making the imaginative journey into the heart of the boy whose parents are getting divorced. Through sharing poems, students can learn to take one another seriously as writers *and* human beings.

But poetry can also *expand* the community. It can take us beyond the classroom—whether that means listening to voices from an inner city playground or the corporate boardroom, to the patient or the doctor, the convict or the prison guard. The range of contemporary poetry, in particular, enables us to hear about the food lines and the shelters, Native American reservations and Japanese- American internment camps, about truck drivers, short-order cooks, and factory workers; we can hear from migrant workers and Buddhist monks, from beauty parlors and grocery stores, the hospitals and the nursing homes. Some of these voices are bound to be new to us. Through the immediate, visceral, memorable language of poetry we can feel both our differences and commonalities.

It may not always be easy to listen. Some of my students, as well as their teacher, have balked at the criticism, the anger, the pain in some of these voices—even the pride. But if we are writing poems about our *own* hurts and joys and needs at the same time, we may find ourselves entering into the feelings of others more easily than we'd have expected.

Because poets are constantly consulting their emotions and physical sensations, they can often break through the conventional attitudes and language that say "Everything's fine. And if it's not, just look the other way." Or, equally, the conventionality that says, "No one has the right to celebrate so blatantly! There's such a thing as appropriate behavior." I've started off a lot of courses lately with Naomi Shihab Nye's poem "Eye-to-Eye," because it urges the students and me to risk crossing some borders[1]:

> *Please forgive this interruption.*
> *I am forging a career,*
> *a delicate enterprise*
> *of eyes. Yours included.*
> *We will meet at the corner,*
> *you with your sack lunch,*
> *me with my guitar.*
> *We will be wearing our famous street faces,*
> *anonymous as trees.*
> *Suddenly you will see me,*
> *you will blink, hesitant,*
> *then realize I have not looked away.*
> *For one brave second*
> *we will stare*
> *openly*
> *from borderless skins.*

This is my salary.
There are no days off.

I preface this reading with an exercise in which the class and I without saying a word arrange ourselves in a circle according to eye color. Then we discuss what this was like—staring into so many pairs of eyes and using only gestures or physical contact to communicate. Months later, when they've learned to "give" poems aloud to one another with their eyes as well as their voices, I remind them of this first day of class, and we revisit the poem in the light of what we've learned about one another and what voices we've encountered that were hard for us to hear.

Every school has its own uncrossed borders. And we all have different ideas of what subjects are "political" (read "risky"). When I took my senior class of mostly white, middle-class students to a poetry workshop with the creative writing class at Trenton High School- mostly black and Latino students –we two teachers, one black and one white, found that the question, "What things make you angry or worried," produced quite different answers from each group. My students were angry about pollution of the environment—but mostly in a very general sense. The Trenton High students were angry at drugs and crime in the streets that they used to get to school.

So when, to follow up this visit, I asked my class to write a "political poem," I wasn't surprised to encounter a lot of resistance. I myself had never written anything I considered a political poem. I wasn't sure I knew what one was.

But I want to describe the ensuing struggle, because I hope you'll try incorporating a "political unit" into your poetry work—even if you call it something else!

Monday, first deadline: "I hate my poem. It really sucks." "Yeah, mine's the worst thing I ever wrote. It's all clichés. It doesn't say anything." "This is so dumb. Why are we doing it?"

Wednesday, second drafts: "There's only one good line in the whole thing. But Sam's isn't bad."

Thursday, read-aloud deadline: "Pass." "Pass." "Okay, I'll read mine, but it's awful. You guys are gonna laugh . . ." "I like it. You talked to your fear like Joy Harjo does in her poem." "You know, it sounded real—like it wasn't just an assignment." Me: "So maybe we each need to choose a technique we liked from those 'political' poems we read in the packet and try using it. Let's list some of those poems on the board and see what you liked in them. . . . Look at how the repetition works in Harjo's poem. Remember how Robert Bly says, 'If you like a line you wrote, say it again! Don't waste it.'"

And then the following week, Sarah comes bounding into class waving a piece of paper in my face. "I know it's late," she said, "but I didn't think I could do one at all. For the longest time I couldn't think of anything to write about. I'm just not a political person. And you said it had to be something based on *our own experience*. But then the other day I was looking at the family tree that hangs in our hall, and I realized this girl with the silver chain must have been my age when she died in the Holocaust—and the poem just came, all at once."

Girl of My People

> *There is a girl who hangs*
> *   from my family tree.*
> *She is limp and blue, and slightly*
> *   charred.*
> *She has been there for fifty years.*
>
> *There is a girl who swings*
> *   from my family tree.*
> *She once was pale, and odd,*
> *   and blue-eyed;*
> *But she now dangles, her eyes red*
> *   and her face grey—*
>
> *There is a star that hangs*
> *   next to the girl.*
> *It is blue, and silky, and looks like*
> *   expensive ink.*
> *Funny, the rope*
> *   around her neck,*

and the star
            above her head
    are made from the same thread.

There is a girl who hangs
        from my family tree.
In my hallway.
She always catches my eye.
Funny, how you can't just ignore a body.

There is a chain around that girl's neck.
It is silver
            with a charm.
It too is slightly charred.

On the silver chain that hangs,

                        with a rope,

around that girl's neck,
There are words,
        and I can read them,
Only I usually don't.

The words that I read,
        only sometimes,
Speak to her God:
        "Baruch Atah!"
Call to her God,
                        from a silver chain,
        around a dead girl's neck.

Funny, those words are carved at the bottom
Of the same tree she hangs from.

There is a tree,
        my family tree,
That grows in my hallway, and it too
        is slightly charred.

Charred from the generations of fire,
    Before that Girl.

Charred from the generations of fire,
    That killed that Girl.

And charred from the fires,
    After that Girl,
That still Burn.

Funny, how you can't just put out a fire.

For me, Sarah's poem was a much-needed confirmation—that sometimes you can teach from your own weakness and ignorance. You think about why writing a political poem would be hard for you—what kinds of knowledge, stimuli, examples, repertoire of literary techniques, would *you* need? Then you try to make these elements available to your students, sit back, gnaw your fingernails, and wait.

As a result of attending four Waterloo Poetry Festivals (see note 5, chap. 11) and pursuing the poems I encountered there into more widely ranging anthologies than our school had been using, I became aware of the growing diversity and outspokenness of contemporary American poets. I learned to *feel* issues that in the past I'd only thought about, and I got a start on thinking about issues I hadn't known *were* issues. So I was able to put together packets of political poetry by Carolyn Forché,[2] Rita Dove,[3] Joy Harjo,[4] Quincy Troupe,[5] Lucille Clifton,[6] Jimmy Santiago Baca,[7] Philip Levine,[8] Li-Young Lee,[9] Marie Howe,[10] Claribel Alegría,[11] Michael Harper,[12] Yehuda Amichai[13]—as well as poets I already knew and loved like Adrienne Rich,[14] Mark Doty,[15] Muriel Rukeyser,[16] May Swenson,[17] and Denise Levertov.[18] A request from our religion department for Holocaust poetry led me to Primo Levi, Irena Klepfisz, Dan Pagis, and Yevgeny Yevtushenko,[19] the first three of whom I found in a new anthology edited by Carolyn Forché, *Poetry of Witness.*[20] And as I read these poets, I thought about poets from the past who might be interesting to read in such a context: Yeats, Auden, Anna Ahkmatova, Blake, Shelley, and the wonderful Turkish poet Nazim Hikmet.[21]

I was excited about creating packets of these poets for my seniors and juniors in the poetry course. But when I asked the class, "How many people consider yourselves political?" no one raised a hand. They expressed scorn for politicians, boredom or bewilderment with newspapers, and a rather confused sense of geography. They did possess some theoretical knowledge of Federalism, the causes of the Civil War, and Brown vs. the Board of Education, but along with this a conviction that "one individual can't make a difference." One senior boy said resignedly, "It doesn't really matter. We've got to get into the right college, then grad school, then a corrupting job where we can earn enough to give our kids the kind of life we've had." Many heads nodded fatalistically. In another school, in another kind of community, the specifics might have been different, but I suspect the sense of helplessness would have been the same.

So I tried again. "Forget 'political' if you find the term meaningless. Think instead about power—and powerlessness. When have you, personally, experienced a sense of powerlessness?"

They talked for a while about the authority of parents and teachers, fate, college admissions officers, referees, standardized tests, drivers' tests, speed traps and police officers. They did have a gut sense, within the limits of the narrow circle many of us live in. Then I tried to push out the edges a little: Was there any group of living creatures, human or animal, that they felt was also powerless, and that they themselves had some personal interest in, even some actual experience with?

I explained, to fill the long silence, that having been to Haiti by myself fifteen years ago and spent most of my week there with a native teenage guide, who took me home to meet his mother and girlfriend and told me which of the children who flocked after us were deserving of my dimes, I now felt a connection to Haiti and its affairs; I read any article I saw on it, sought out Haitian novels and art, sent checks for aid, and wrote letters for Amnesty International protesting civil rights abuses there. "While none of this constitutes any very active engagement or self-sacrifice, each cause I can learn to care about through some personal contact widens my circle a little bit and makes me feel less helpless."

I thought if I could lead each student to define an area of personal concern, she could start by finding out more about that area and acquainting the rest of us with what she learned. Then she could write a poem about it, which would mean exploring some feelings that might, till now, have registered only subconsciously.

Gradually a few students' hands were going up. One girl had been to a particular Caribbean island many times and had grown aware of the local inhabitants' anger at American tourists. It made her feel guilty, seeing the differences between how most of them lived and how she did. She felt uncomfortable being waited on by them; it was their island, after all. But she enjoyed the snorkeling, and they needed her family's money . . . so it wouldn't make sense to stop going there, would it? I recommended as a starting place Jamaica Kincaid's complicated and articulate anger in her book about growing up in Antigua, *A Small Place*.[22]

Another student had seen the film *Dances with Wolves* and had asked his history teacher why they didn't study more about Native American history. He could remember his third-grade class giving money to an Indian kid. He wondered if teenagers from a reservation ever got scholarships to private schools. I told him about a project in which prep school teachers (my brother, for one) went out to the University of New Mexico to work with promising Navajo eighth-graders, some of whom would be offered places and tuition at private schools back East. I also told him there were struggling schools on the reservations that needed support. And I mentioned Matthiessen's *Spirit of Crazy Horse*[23] and Mary Crow Dog's *Lakota Woman*.[24]

I also invited the class to brainstorm together a list of elements that make society and the human condition absurd—just to get them to take a fresh look at their assumptions. They came up with:

> 20,000 years of male-dominated society
> mixing religion with government
> allowing lawyers to run the country
> Elvis sightings
> good manners
> carnivores
> religious fanatics
> how death can come so fast and take away someone but the pain lasts
>   so long
> sports stars' salaries
> people not voting

industry running government

SATs

the entertainment industry

lapdogs

fear of death but infatuation with it

paying $76,000 for a car

extremes created by class structure

funerals and weddings

violent solutions

women

bureaucracies

schools

I wondered what a list drawn up by Trenton High School's writing class would have looked like, or by a school in a small, Midwestern town—what items in common, what differences. This present class's list, with its combination of genuine angst and tongue-in-cheek humor, led me to show them some surrealist and absurdist poets—André Breton, Charles Simic, Lawrence Ferlinghetti, Russell Edson. These turned out to be more popular among the boys, while many of the girls were drawn to feminist poets, some of whom had written witty political satire—Margaret Atwood, Marge Piercy, Lucille Clifton, Adrienne Rich, Joy Harjo, Sharon Olds, Diane Wakoski. So, drawing on these poets and others, I put together packets of poems covering a range of issues having to do with power and powerlessness.

Worried that the numerous historical and political allusions in some of these poems—to say nothing of geography!—would slow my readers down, and therefore turn them off, I asked everyone to put check marks next to any names and events that were unfamiliar; we'd sort them out together. I put at the front of the packet the contemporary American poems, with which I felt they could build up some momentum, though I realized with a pang that events which were "contemporary" to me—the Civil Rights movement, Vietnam, Stonewall, AIM (American Indian Movement)—were ancient history. To keep the focus on power, I introduced the packet with an in-class exercise on that word and a homework journal-assignment in which they could explore their personal experiences with power—positive and negative—from childhood up to the present. Since they had just finished

working with their third-grade partners on children's poetry, many wrote
interestingly about the power and lack of power they remembered feeling
as children. When we shared our writings, our definitions of "political"
began, gradually, to broaden. Students started to feel they might actually be
able to write a political poem. "Are eating disorders maybe to do with
power?" a girl ventured; we plunged into a discussion of advertising, the
media . . .

I asked them to organize their packet of poems from favorites to least
favorites. "How to Watch Your Brother Die" by Michael Lassell and "The
Colonel," Carolyn Forché's prose poem about El Salvador, were very popular.
So was "Bleeding," May Swenson's chilling dialogue between the knife and
the cut. So was Joy Harjo's poem addressed to fear, "I Give You Back." But
opinions varied enough so nearly every poem had a defender, and again, I
felt the circle widening. Auden's "In Memory of W.B. Yeats" was less popular
than most of the other poems, due to its greater difficulty and its remote-
ness, both cultural and historical. But the issue it raised of whether a poem
could "make something happen" interested the class. So did the question,
raised in an article by poet David Mura, of whether a political poem could,
through the poet's honesty in confronting his own failings, transcend propa-
ganda and self-righteousness.[25] By now we were defining "political poem" as
any poem that dealt with inequities of power from a particular point of
view.

The students were pleased that most of the political poems they read
were rooted in the poet's personal experience. "Did Muriel Rukeyser really
go to jail? Was Levertov really in Vietnam? How did Carolyn Forché get to
have dinner with that Salvadoran general? This Turkish guy [Nazim Hikmet]
must have spent most of his *life* in jail! Quincy Troupe gives poetry workshops in Sing Sing? They felt as though they were entering the "real world,"
though they also began to worry, "How can I write a political poem?
Nothing's ever happened to me." So we were back to discussing "What's
political?" "Look at Sharon Olds's poem 'On the Subway,' I suggested.[26] "She's
doing this perfectly ordinary thing—just riding the subway—but suddenly
that ride becomes a whole series of hard questions for her about power."
"Shouldn't she show both sides?" someone asked. "That wouldn't be a poem,
that would be an essay," someone else shot back. "And besides, would Olds
have the right to speak for the black boy?" These were issues I had struggled
with in my own poems; it was helpful to listen to the class working them

out. "Even if nobody reads it," I said, "writing a political poem is a healthy action, as long as it's an honest poem. You'll have had to feel some pain, anger, empathy. You'll have had to relate to something or someone outside yourself, and probably ask yourself a hard question or two."

The students did, finally, all manage to find an issue to write about. Their poems included a Korean-American girl's attack on her father's enforcement of patriarchy at home; an Indian girl's guilty lament over not being with her relatives in India during the current religious riots and watching the television reports instead; an African American boy's refusal to blend in with his white school friends; and the following piece on the Gulf War by an outspoken Jewish girl:

quiet night, january 1991

>   i shiver under three blankets
>   with my knees tucked against my breasts
>   as the bombs scream down upon
>   a sleeping Baghdad
>
>   my television set glows like a
>   surrealist nightmare in the darkness
>   and as dan rather points clumsily
>   to a map of the middle east
>   i wish that the countries really did float
>   flat and serene
>   a sea of pink yellow green and lavender
>
>   but in the smattering of stars and dots
>   cities once stood
>   before the buildings buckled into dust
>   before smoke was burnt in the bone
>   before the war
>
>   freedom
>   liberation
>   new world order

these words have wedged themselves
          in the back of my throat-cave
                    choking me as images flash across the screen
of an iraqi woman flailing in the gravel by the roadside
          her womb aching and burning
                    for the child that lies broken and
crusted with blood
          under a heap of shrapnel   it was a
                    "smart bomb" they say

outside my window
          the american flag
                    flashes like cold steel in the moonlight

I was particularly moved by Shara's empathy with Arab women because she also wrote a poem about identifying with Holocaust victims:

close your eyes to pity

the jew-girl is angry
she stares at the frozen image
at the mouth
this dark twisted hollow
and at the closed fist shaking
          rattling six million
six million   *rattling, clanging,*
banging
as the swastika snaps into spears of fire
that char her skin and leave it smoking

the jew-girl is angry
thirty-five thousand were marched to babi yar
and thirty-five thousand tottered on the edge of an abyss
no time to scream only the silent wailing
trapped in the mirror of a child's eye as they exploded
plunging ever deeper and finally

the wet smacking of flesh against bloody flesh as they
hit bottom

the jew-girl is angry
she pulls this head this mouth this hatred deep
into her chest and howls
as it sucks her dry

As we listened to these poems being read aloud, I felt the circle expand. A very talented sculptor, a girl in whom I felt the cynic and the idealist constantly at war, wrote:

It's hard to be
politically correct.
You can't eat,
wear clothes,
sleep without
guilt,
or walk
on the grass
without crushing
someone half-way
around the world
who happens to live
under your ignorant
foot.

The one African American boy in the class had initially seen himself, a football captain, as being out of place among this rather artsy theater crowd. In a journal entry he compared this situation to his arrival at the school four years earlier, the only black student in his grade; gradually he'd won acceptance and popularity on his own terms. This recollection gave him courage. He introduced us to the poems of Claude McKay and helped establish rapport when our class joined the writing class at Trenton High for a day. Borrowing a line from poet Gerald Stern[27] for his opening, he wrote:

I could live like that,
pale skin, blond hair and blue eyes,
have control of the country
and think myself superior to others.

I could live like that,
not being harassed and suspected,
not being feared and hated
because of the color of my skin.

But why would I want to live like that?
Why give up my strong, rich background,
unable to be broken or beaten,
determined to fight back and win?

Why leave behind my brother and sister,
the suffering and sorrow we shared,
and give up my golden-brown skin
for a pale, transparent color?

The most controversial poem, and the one most admired by the class, was the work of a gay student, who was in the process of coming out at school (though not at home). He had admired the poem by Michael Lassell called "How to Watch Your Brother Die."[28] Many of us had found that "stealing" a technique from a poem we liked was helpful in getting us started, especially when dealing with "dangerous" feelings. Borrowing Lassell's device of an opening "if" clause for each stanza and a series of energizing imperative verbs helped "Matt" a lot. The final line in his original version had to be rewritten if the poem were to get into the school literary magazine, and, gritting his teeth, he rewrote it:

Tell-tale Signs

If you wake up one morning
and find me next to you on the pillow,
do not be shocked.

Call me your brother,
your old friend,
your new friend.
Do not call me your lover.
They would not approve.

If we should go out tonight, you must follow the rules:
Do not allow your voice to quiver when you ask for a table for two,
and do not let your tongue roll into a lisp
or hang your wrist limply.
Do not hold my hand
or sit too close to me.
Do not trace the skin beneath my jeans
or put your hand over mine
and do not try to
kiss me.
These are tell-tale signs.

Or if you want to forget the rules
for once
and come with me,
do it. But
we can't go to church
because it's against God
and we can't go to your house
because it's immoral
and we can't go to Georgia
because it's illegal.

But we can sit on a bench
in a midnight park for hours
and kiss.

Since Matt had raised the topic in class and his peers were sympathetic, I shared with them my political poem, one I'd written about a former student, though I hadn't finished it yet:

Tasting the Word

One of them was my student once,
grubby and hyper: he had to own my class,
talked us to death. (The word 'gay'
fluttered around his head, just out of reach.
At night it roosted in corners.)
Now home is the futon where his lover
brushes sleep and blond curls from his eyes.
Up late reunifying Germany,
he's hungry for angel hair and peppers.
He slips in their favorite tape,
lights candles, and plays that he's cooking
cereal for the two-year-old. Both dream
of the little girl who hugs their waist each time
they visit "Case 3214." Things aren't so good there.
The foster mother drinks a lot. They picture
bruises, and bathing that small body,
talcum between the toes. . . .

How much of "parenthood" is fantasy, anyway?
Just a word, I float it off my tongue
as I help them clean up. The word drifts
into the suds, a little wafer of light
losing itself in steam. But it sounds heavy,
like German. "Is your child in order?"
I once read on a sign there.
Are we in order? What if I had two fathers?
My tongue flicks my teeth, tasting the soft "th,"
the "ah" deep in my throat—"fathers"—the final
growl and hiss. But they are gentle
together. From them I might have learned
generosity and to say what I want.
To be brave with power tools and strangers.
They are makers and healers,
and better at child's play than I. . . .

In the process of reading, hearing, writing, and performing their political poems, some of the students had moved out of themselves—or reached deeper into themselves. Now they wanted to *do* something. I think this is where so often education fails, leaving student and teacher alike asking, "Is that all?" Learning comes to feel purely theoretical; it "makes nothing happen." I didn't have an immediate solution. We did get our school Amnesty International chapter to help us organize an assembly on the raping of women and girls in the Balkan camps; one of my students read the poem she'd written about this, and others read from personal accounts they'd found by some of the women prisoners. We were surprised at how many people stopped at the tables we'd set up to write letters of protest. Several students joined the Community Council's efforts to sensitize the school to sexual harassment, in preparation for developing an official policy. A few girls joined a march in New York to raise money for AIDS research. I privately resolved to ask our Alumni Office to rethink their annual Career Day and find more alumni engaged in jobs that contributed to redressing social wrongs. Our present students badly needed role models close to home.

I want my school and classroom to be expansive, inclusive circles. And to work to make this happen seems to me a political action, perhaps the most immediate and personal one that we—and our students—can take. Recently I ran across four lines from a poem by nineteenth century poet Edwin Markham[29]:

> He drew a circle that shut me out—
> Heretic, rebel, a thing to flout.
> But Love and I had the wit to win:
> We drew a circle that took him in!

In Markham's poem the "I" that allies itself with love to expand the circle can be read as the empathizing imagination. The poet's imagination. And that force, as I am trying to help my student poets see, can re-draw their world. If we can trust our own hearts to speak, each of us as reader and writer has the capacity to "touch a level in the psyche where we're all the same."

Notes

1. Naomi Shihab Nye, "Eye-to-Eye" in *Words under the Words* (Portland, OR: Far Corner Books, 1995) 11.

Some Poems I Have Used in Packets of Political Poetry

2. Carolyn Forché, "The Colonel" in *The Country between Us*
(New York: Harper & Row, 1981) 16.

3. Rita Dove, "Crab-Boil" in *Grace Notes* (New York: W. W. Norton, 1989) 13.

4. Joy Harjo, "I Give You Back" *in She Had Some Horses* (see note 9, chap. 9). See also video, *The Power of the Word*, note 1, chap. 1.

5. Quincy Troupe, "After Hearing a Radio Announcement, a comment on Some Conditions: 1978" in *Weather Reports* (see note 1, chap. 9).

6. Lucille Clifton, "in the inner city," 15 (see note 4, chap. 3); and "i am accused of tending to the past . . ." in *quilting* (Brockport, NY: BOA Editions, 1991) 7.

7. Jimmy Santiago Baca, "El Gato," on *Language of Life* video, program # 6 (and printed in the teacher's guide) (see note 8, chap. 9).

8. Philip Levine, "Coming Close" in *What Work Is*, 5 (see note 6, chap. 9). See also video *Poetry Heaven* and teacher's guide, note 8, chap. 9.

9. Li-Young Lee, "The Interrogation" in *The City in Which I Love You* (Brockport NY: BOA Editions, 1990), 33–34. See also the video *Poetry Heaven*.

10. Marie Howe, "A Certain Light" in *What the Living Do* (New York: W. W. Norton, 1998) 44–45. See also the video *Poetry Heaven*.

11. Claribel Alegría, "From the Bridge" in *Woman of the River*, trans. D. J. Flakoll (Pittsburgh: University of Pittsburgh Press, 1989) 11–17. This is a bilingual edition, so you can ask students who speak Spanish to read parts of the poem aloud for the class. See also *The Language of Life* video, program # 4.

12. Michael S. Harper, "A Mother Speaks: The Algiers Motel Incident, Detroit" and "Nightmare Begins Responsibility," both in *Images of Kin: New and Selected Poems* (Urbana and Chicago: University of Illinois Press, 1977) 204 and 57. See also *Language of Life* video, program # 7.

13. Yehuda Amichai, "The Diameter of the Bomb" in *Selected Poetry*, trans. Chana Bloch and Stephen Mitchell (New York: Harper & Row, 1986) 118. See also the video, *Poetry Heaven.*

14. Adrienne Rich, "Rape" in *The Fact of a Doorframe, Poems New and Selected 1950–1984* (New York:W. W. Norton, 1984) 172.

_____ "Prospective Immigrants Please Note" in *Collected Early Poems: 1950–1970* (New York: W. W. Norton, 1993).

_____ (Dedications) XIII from "An Atlas of the Difficult World" in *An Atlas of the Difficult World Poems 1988–1991* (New York: W. W. Norton, 1991) 25–26. See also the *Language of Life* video, program # 7

15. Mark Doty, "Atlantis" in *Atlantis: Poems* (New York: HarperCollins, 1995) 49–54. See also the video, *Poetry Heaven.*

16. Muriel Rukeyser, "Myth" in *A Muriel Rukeyser Reader*, ed. Jan Heller Levi (New York: W. W. Norton, 1994) 252.

17. May Swenson, "Bleeding" in *Nature, Poems Old and New* (New York: Houghton Mifflin, 1994) 64.

18. Denise Levertov, "What Were They Like?" in *The Sorrow Dance* (New York: New Directions, 1966) 84.

19. Yevgeny Yevtushenko, "Babiy Yar" in *Selected Poems,* trans. Robin Milner-Gulland and Peter Levi, S. J. (Baltimore: Penguin Books, 1967) 82–84.

20. Forché, *Poetry of Witness* (see note 4, chap. 11).

21. Nazim Hikmet, "On Living" and "Angina Pectoris" in *Selected Poetry*, trans. Randy Blasing and Mutlu Konuk (New York: Persea Books, 1986) 97–99 and 101.

22. Jamaica Kincaid, *A Small Place* (New York: Penguin/New American Library, 1988).

23. Peter Matthiessen, *In the Spirit of Crazy Horse* (New York: Viking, 1983).

24. Mary Crow Dog and Richard Erdoes, *Lakota Woman* (New York: Grove Weidenfeld, 1990).

25. David Mura (see note 3, chap. 1).

26. Sharon Olds, "On the Subway," 5 (see note 1, chap. 11).

27. Gerald Stern, "Saying the First Words" in *The Paradise Poems* (New York: Vintage/Random House, 1982) 37.

28. Michael Lassell, "How to Watch Your Brother Die" in *Poets for Life: Seventy-six Poets Respond to AIDS* (see note 4, chap. 11).

29. Edwin Markham, "Outwitted" in *The Best Loved Poems of the American People*, ed. Hazel Felleman (New York: Doubleday, 1936).

Appendix

For Further Reading

Addonizio, Kim and Laux, Dorianne. The Poet's Companion: A Guide to the Pleasures of Writing Poetry. New York: W. W. Norton, 1997. Two poets who have taught in high schools and universities discuss the process and craft of writing poetry. Each chapter ends with helpful exercises that you, as a teacher, can try yourself as well as use in the classroom. The first section, about one third of the book, discusses subjects to write about. There is even a chapter on sentence structure, that employs traditional grammatical terms and could help improve student writing in any genre. The book ends with some twenty-minute exercises, and good lists of anthologies, books on poetry, bookstores (including some online), poetry magazines, and CD-ROMs.

Collom, Jack. Moving Windows: Evaluating the Poetry Children Write. New York: Teachers & Writers Collaborative, 1985. A poet-in-the-schools, Collom has written a book that addresses one of the thorniest questions that classroom teachers face: how to evaluate a student's poem. He bases his suggestions on the full texts of more than three hundred poems written by students in his workshops, and although these are elementary and junior high school children, the principles apply to the work of older students as well.

Collom, Jack and Noethe, Sheryl. Poetry Everywhere: Teaching Poetry Writing in School and in the Community. New York: Teachers & Writers Collaborative, 1994.

This book contains sixty writing exercises and warm-ups designed for students of all ages; hundreds of sample poems by students, teachers, and published writers, including translations; a chapter on designing poetry units; and a chapter on integrating poetry into the standard English class. The range of examples is particularly wide, and the "Tips on Leading Poetry Sessions" are very helpful.

GENSLER, KINERETH AND NYHART, NINA. THE POETRY CONNECTION: AN ANTHOLOGY OF CONTEMPORARY POEMS WITH IDEAS TO STIMULATE CHILDREN'S WRITING. NEW YORK: TEACHERS & WRITERS COLLABORATIVE, 1978. Two poets-in-the-schools offer "model" poems, including some by children, and suggest ways in which teachers and students might use these poems to get started on their own. While the oldest students mentioned are ninth-graders, the teaching technique and many of the model poems—by W. S. Merwin, May Swenson, Denise Levertov, Stanley Kunitz, etc.—are appropriate for high schoolers.

GOLDBERG, NATALIE. WRITING DOWN THE BONES: FREEING THE WRITER WITHIN AND WILD MIND: LIVING THE WRITER'S LIFE. NEW YORK: QUALITY PAPERBACK BOOK CLUB, 1991. This convenient edition that combines two of Goldberg's books offers practical advice on writing by a poet, novelist, and teacher who draws from her own life and her double "practice" of Zen and writing. The exercises are useful, for both teachers and students of writing.

HUGO, RICHARD. THE TRIGGERING TOWN: LECTURES AND ESSAYS ON POETRY AND WRITING. NEW YORK: W. W. NORTON, 1992. This brief collection of essays on the nature of poetry and the writing process was dedicated by Hugo to "all students of creative writing—and . . . their teachers" and is particularly interesting on the question of how a poem gets started.

JORDAN, JUNE. POETRY FOR THE PEOPLE: A REVOLUTIONARY BLUEPRINT, ED. LAUREN MULLER AND THE POETRY FOR THE PEOPLE COLLECTIVE. NEW YORK: ROUTLEDGE, 1995. Poet and Professor of African American Studies and Women's Studies, Jordan shares her experience of empowering children, college students and adults of many races by helping them "reinvent the canon." She enables them to discover poems and poets that speak for them and their communities, and that give them language with which to make their feelings memorable to others. She demonstrates ways to run multiracial poetry workshops at various age levels, to create and publicize poetry readings for a multilingual community, to train college students to help elementary schoolers enjoy poetry, and to publish student poetry collections. She provides poetry bibliographies that emphasize diversity, and offers samples of her students' poems from their thematic collections, *Poetry in a Time of Genocide, Poetry for the People in a Time of War*, etc.

LAMOTT, ANNE. BIRD BY BIRD: SOME INSTRUCTIONS ON WRITING AND LIFE. NEW YORK: ANCHOR/ DOUBLEDAY, 1994. The novelist offers a witty, anecdotal discussion of the writing life and craft. Her exercises and some of her advice, though focused on fiction rather than poetry, are definitely relevant to high school writers and their teachers. She quotes an old Mel Brooks routine in which the therapist tells the patient, "Listen to your broccoli, and your broccoli will tell you how to eat it." Or, as Lamott says, "You get your intuition back when you make space for it. . . . Rationality squeezes out much that is rich and juicy and fascinating."

LARRICK, NANCY, ED. SOMEBODY TURNED ON A TAP IN THESE KIDS: POETRY AND YOUNG PEOPLE TODAY. NEW YORK: DELACORTE PRESS, 1971. Despite the publication date, this book offers good insights into why poetry—and what kinds of poetry—can be important to adolescents. A collection of essays by poet/teachers past and present, including Eve Merriam and June Jordan as well as two teachers at an all-black inner city school, it contains some strong poems, by published poets and by students, that would reach today's high schoolers, and describes actual classroom practice.

LEHMAN, DAVID, ED. ECSTATIC OCCASIONS, EXPEDIENT FORMS: 65 LEADING CONTEMPORARY POETS SELECT AND COMMENT ON THEIR POEMS. NEW YORK: COLLIER/MACMILLAN, 1987. Each poet presents a poem along with a personal explanation of how the poem's form relates to its content. The forms vary from free verse to traditional and modified sonnets, villanelles, etc. These commentaries offer insights into both process and craft.

LEHMAN, DAVID, SERIES ED. THE BEST AMERICAN POETRY. NEW YORK: SIMON & SCHUSTER. This is a yearly anthology of poems chosen by a different poet each year from literary magazines. The poet also writes an introduction, and these brief essays are some of the most articulate, passionate discussions of poetry around.

LIES, BETTY BONHAM. THE POET'S PEN: WRITING POETRY WITH MIDDLE AND HIGH SCHOOL STUDENTS. ENGLEWOOD, CO: TEACHER IDEAS PRESS, 1993. A high school teacher and poet offers twelve poetry lessons illustrated by some of her students' work, including methods for integrating poetry writing with other parts of the English curriculum. This book makes clear how writing poems can help students improve as writers of other genres such as the expository essay.

MARZAN, JULIO, ED. LUNA, LUNA: CREATIVE WRITING IDEAS FROM SPANISH, LATIN AMERICAN, AND LATINO LITERATURE. NEW YORK: TEACHERS & WRITERS, 1997. These twenty-one lessons by various writer/teachers offer literary models from Spain and the Americas to inspire students from elementary school to college. Contributors include Kenneth Koch, Bill Zavatsky, Naomi Shihab Nye, and Julia Alvarez, and the models range from Pablo Neruda and Federico Garcia Lorca to contemporary poets Sandra Cisneros and Victor Hernandez Cruz.

OSTRIKER, ALICIA. STEALING THE LANGUAGE: THE EMERGENCE OF WOMEN'S POETRY IN AMERICA. BOSTON: BEACON, 1986. Ostriker, a poet and university professor, examines, through her readings of such writers as Rich, Levertov, Bishop, Sexton, Lorde, and Clifton, the ways in which women poets have had to search for new metaphors and revise old myths in order to confront the divided self, the female body, and the traditional assumptions about female creativity.

PADGETT, RON, ED. THE TEACHERS & WRITERS HANDBOOK OF POETIC FORMS. NEW YORK: TEACHERS & WRITERS COLLABORATIVE, 1987. This is a particularly useful handbook because it not only defines seventy-four forms, including rap, insult poem, and blues, gives their origins and history, and provides examples, but also offers advice on how to write in each form.

RUKEYSER, MURIEL. THE LIFE OF POETRY. ASHFIELD, MA: PARIS PRESS, 1996. This book, first published in 1949, explores the role poetry can play in our lives if given half a chance, and, in its range of connections, reflects the remarkable depth and breadth of this activist poet's understanding, from political history and contemporary politics to physics, blues, baseball, advertising, film-making, and the human psyche. It has a foreword by poet Jane Cooper.

STAFFORD, WILLIAM. WRITING THE AUSTRALIAN CRAWL: VIEWS ON THE WRITER'S VOCATION. ANN ARBOR: UNIVERSITY OF MICHIGAN PRESS, 1978.

STAFFORD, WILLIAM. YOU MUST REVISE YOUR LIFE. ANN ARBOR: UNIVERSITY OF MICHIGAN PRESS, 1986. Both these books are part of Michigan's very fine "Poets on Poetry" series. The late William Stafford was one of the most beloved of poets and teachers, and the unpretentiousness, humor, and quiet passion of these two books show why. Both are collections of vignettes, articles, interviews, and some of Stafford's poems that touch on the creative process. They are about reading poems as well as writing them. "A writer," said Stafford, "is not so much someone who has something to say as he is someone who has found a process that will bring about new things he would not have thought of if he had not started to say them."

WOOLRIDGE, SUSAN G. POEMCRAZY: FREEING YOUR LIFE WITH WORDS. NEW YORK: RANDOM HOUSE, 1997. A writer who works for California Poets in the Schools and also leads adult workshops, Woolridge focuses on how to "drop a line into the pool of words around you and within you to begin making poems that express more than words can say." One of those books that makes you want to pick up a pencil and start writing.

Author

Judith Rowe Michaels serves as Artist-in-Residence, K–12, at Princeton Day School and is a poet in the schools for the Geraldine R. Dodge Foundation. Michaels, who earned a Ph.D. in English from Bryn Mawr College, has published poems in many journals, including *Poetry Northwest, Yankee Magazine, New York Quarterly, Columbia Review, Mudfish,* and *Journal of New Jersey Poets.* For the past four summers she has had writing residencies at the Banff Centre for the Arts in Alberta, Canada. In 1995 she won a New Jersey State Council on the Arts Fellowship in Poetry and recently won first prize in the national competition, "Presenting Poetry and Prose." Her students have consistently won poetry-writing awards in state competitions, and she has adjudicated manuscripts for state and county poetry festivals and workshops. Michaels has also served during the past twenty years as a school coordinator and sometimes as a writer/researcher with Lincoln Center's Summer Institute in aesthetic education.

Risking Intensity

Composed by Electronic Imaging in Veljovic and ExPonto.
Typeface used on the cover was Caslon Antique.
Calligraphy by Barbara Yale-Read.
Printed by Versa Press on 60-lb. Opaque Offset paper.